MATT McCONNELL
WITH JO GAMVROS

Lourinhã

IBERIAN AND MEDITERRANEAN DISHES TO SHARE

Hardie Grant
BOOKS

Foreword

BY SIMON JOHNSON

From the early days of my business I was fortunate enough to develop a friendship with Matt and Jo through the camaraderie of the hospitality industry and a vision that a number of restaurateurs and providores embraced: one of quality produce inspired by a generosity of sharing, one of provenance, knowledge and of change for good. We were all younger and wanting to make a difference, and the marketplace was embracing change; it was time to raise the standards and challenge the tradition of what dining in Australia was all about. As a providore, I have always been amazed at how an industry that is so competitive forges so many lasting friendships.

In those early days we would all gather for the annual Noosa Food & Wine Festival, where Matt was on the pans at Berardo's and share stories of produce-inspired travels from far corners of the world, and talk about the ideas we brought back that have shaped the way we eat today. Gone are the doilies, the lace tablecloths and rich dishes that make you feel like you need to reach for a bottle of antacid pills.

These gatherings were not just about the food, they were an opportunity to help and support others in the hospitality industry, which can be fickle and very unforgiving if anything goes wrong (as often happens): a lack of funds, loss of focus or a bad review. What I admire about Matt and Jo is their unwavering vision and determination, along with focusing on what counts in the restaurant industry, where patron satisfaction and staff wellbeing are key to the longevity of any good establishment.

It was at one of these gatherings that Matt and the vivacious Jo were waxing lyrical about their dream of a new Melbourne dining experience. They had been inspired by their travels in Spain, Jo's family in nearby Naples and the market culture in these places, which centres around serving good produce with the warm hospitality of a small, family-run bar, and they were keen to create a place reminiscent of this Mediterranean way of life.

Welcome to *Lourinhã*, and the new and exciting era of bar culture that has spawned because of Matt and Jo's success and vision: an era where produce is king and simplicity is key, along with a place to eat that is welcoming, relaxed and friendly. For Matt and Jo, it is about the experience and the complete package, as the front-of-house service has to be as good as the food. They have changed the way we view our local bar.

I have many fond memories of sitting at the bar, enjoying a glass and saying to Jo, 'Just ask Matt to send out his favourite dishes', as he is often under the pump in the kitchen but never too busy to give a welcoming wave. It's that friendly attitude and generosity – along with plates of food that make you feel good – that make Bar Lourinhã what it is.

I'm lucky enough to travel to Melbourne regularly, and it's always a joy after a busy day to grab a glass of wine and share a few dishes that Matt has created. And it's made all the more special by the welcoming smile from Jo as you walk in the door. It reminds me of those family-run tapas and pintxo bars that I feel so at home in when travelling through Spain, but with a wonderful Australian feel that is quintessentially Matt and Jo.

COMIDA
BAR
Lourinhã
TAPAS
Local organic olives 8
Almonds & spice 8
House pickles 8
Bacalhau toast .... 4 ea.
Boquerone, mojo picon & fried bread .... 4 ea.
Salt grilled shishito peppers .... 4 ea.
Jamon croqueta .... 4 ea.
RACIONES
Yellowtail kingfish 'pancetta' & lemon oil 20
Grilled octopus, corn & ancho 25
Cucumbers, stretched curd & dill 16
Hierloom tomatoes, ink & basil 16
Spiced chickpea & spinach 16
Roasted mushrooms & garlic cream 17
'Cecina' & poached tomato 22
Grilled lambs tongue, peppers & almond 24
Crisp chicken, watercress & salsa picante 29
QUESO
RABBIT
WAGYU
BAR

Contents

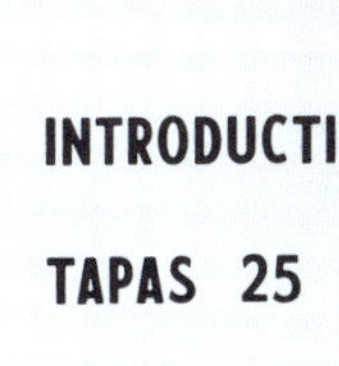

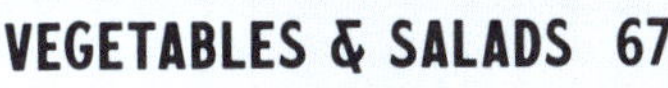

Introduction

Twenty years ago, we opened Bar Lourinhã to share our love of Mediterranean and Iberian flavours, and our belief that true hospitality comes from the heart. We also wanted to highlight the culture of the bar, which revolves around enjoying what's good in the moment, with no expectations of what will be on offer.

Today, it's easier to explain what we like about bar dining, but, when we first started talking about opening our own place, we had lots of ideas but no clear picture of what we wanted to do. We'd both worked in hospitality for years – Matt as a chef and Jo working front of house – and so we knew the things that we did and didn't like but, in Australia at the time, there was no culture of bar dining. There were restaurants, bars, pubs and cafés. Nobody was doing what we wanted to do, so we went in search of it ourselves.

For us, the adventure really started with our first trip to Spain in 1997. We had taken over the dining room at the Napier Hotel in Fitzroy and created a bar menu, which we found more fun and interesting than what you could do with a restaurant menu but didn't think it was the kind of thing you could base a business on. And then we flew to Europe, visited Barcelona for the first time and stumbled across a bar that made us start thinking that maybe we could do it after all.

We found La Pineda via the most delicious smell that turned out to be freshly baked empanadas filled with fresh and cured tuna. We followed the smell through a door to this beautiful dark, cool space. A father-and-son team ran the place and they greeted us, gestured to where we should sit and then brought out some empanadas, a handful of olives, banderillas, house-made pickles and a bit of cheese.

The service was beautiful. We felt completely welcome though we didn't speak the language and we were served exactly what the locals would eat. We liked its style, its smell, its look. We wanted that for our place.

The other thing that interested us on this first trip to Spain was the relationship between bars and the markets. It seems like every town and city in Spain has at least one market surrounded by clusters of bars in the nearby streets that all serve what's local and available from the market that day. This direct relationship between the market and what was being served in bars was a real eye-opener for us.

There was one bar called Tasca Angel near a market in Valencia. It was a no-seat, standing-only kind of place run by two brothers. Tasca Angel was famous for its sardines, which they quickly grilled and served with a green sauce. On the days that they had sardines, the crowd would be three-deep. We joined the crowd and the sardines were amazing so we decided to go back again the next day. But this time there was no crowd. The reason? No sardines at the market that day. Frozen sardines were probably an option, but they would never do it because the whole experience, the whole reason for the bar's popularity, was all about the freshest, best ingredient.

When we came back to Australia, it seemed the gulf between what we wanted to do and what was happening in Melbourne was wider than ever. Matt went back to the restaurant world but, after our experience in Europe, found the formality of that kind of dining restrictive. Also, it wasn't the way we liked to eat and if you don't like to eat that way, how can you be passionate about that kind of cooking?

Matt took a job in Noosa, a seaside town in Queensland. The place was called Berardo's and it served Mediterranean food with a Spanish leaning. Moving north completely changed our lifestyle from going out all night to getting up at 5.30 am to meet the fishermen to see what was available that day. It was the first time that we had direct access to fresh produce like that, to form a relationship with the supplier. In Melbourne, everything used to arrive by delivery van and so you were always three-arms'-length from the producer. The way we were able to source ingredients at Berardo's reminded us of the way people did it in Europe. The seed had been planted. We saw that it was possible to operate like that in Australia too.

After three years in Noosa we wanted to move back to Melbourne to open our own business, but had to work out what it was that we were going to do. What we'd seen in Europe – and Spain in particular – spoke to us, so in 2006 we left Australia to spend a year over there on a fact-finding mission, focusing on the bars, the little restaurants and the food being sold in the markets.

Our first stop was Naples where Jo has family. We'd spent a lot of time in Naples in the past, staying with Jo's great-aunties who were both amazing cooks and had properties in the country outside the city: one at Valle Agricola, the other at Ciorlano. They grew and preserved a lot of their own food.

In planning the trip we'd been very focused on the Spanish and Portuguese legs in terms of our future business, so we hadn't thought that Naples would have the major influence on us that it did. It wasn't so much in terms of specific recipes that would end up on our menu, but in the attitude to ingredients and a particular service style.

We loved the way that people talked about the ingredients they used. Zia Lina would talk to us about the ingredients for a simple salad, where they'd come from, where and when to pick or buy them and the whole time she would be working, shredding freshly picked tomatoes and basil leaves, preparing creamy buffalo mozzarella from a farm that was 20 minutes away by car, thick coarse salt from the land and some olives. And then, like magic, there's a beautiful salad in front of you.

This is where the whole idea of freshness and simplicity that underpins what we do at Bar Lourinhã comes from: the incredible insight we were given from Jo's aunties into a little home kitchen in Naples that relied solely on the seasonal and the preserved.

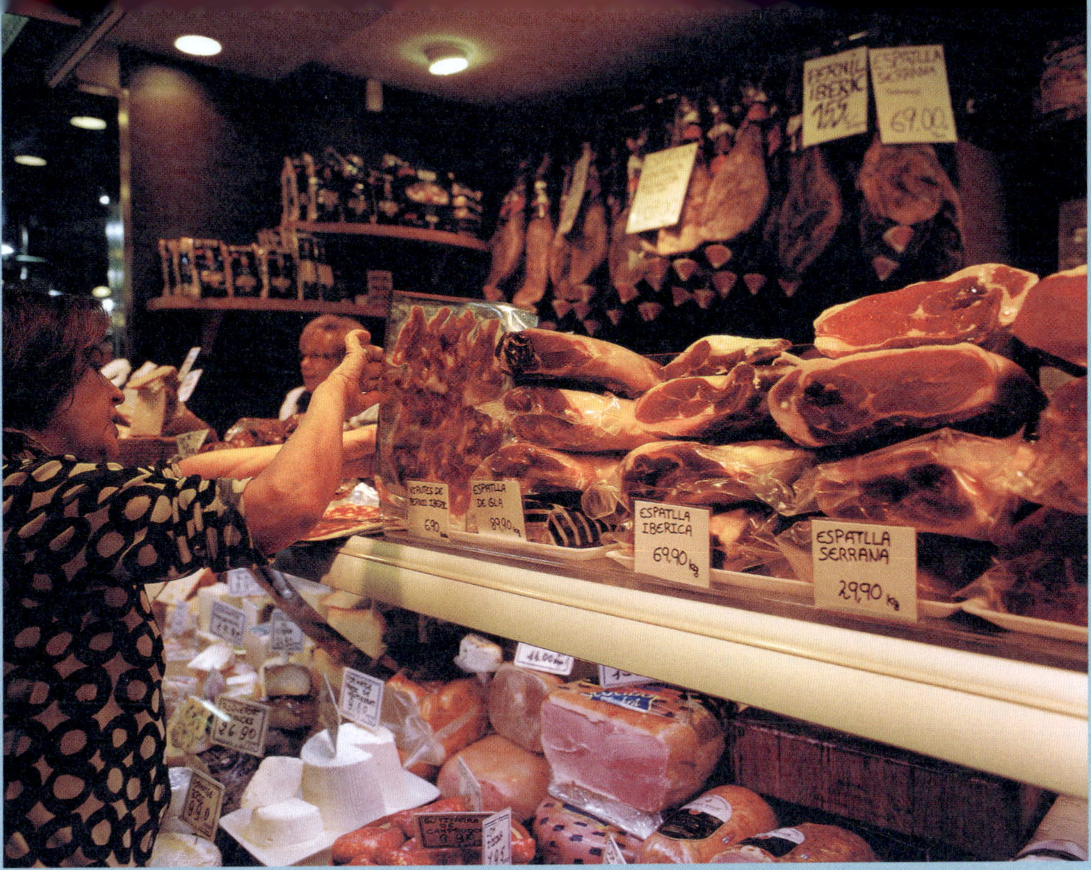
ESPATLLA
IBERICA
69,90 kg
ESPATLLA
SERRANA
29,90 kg

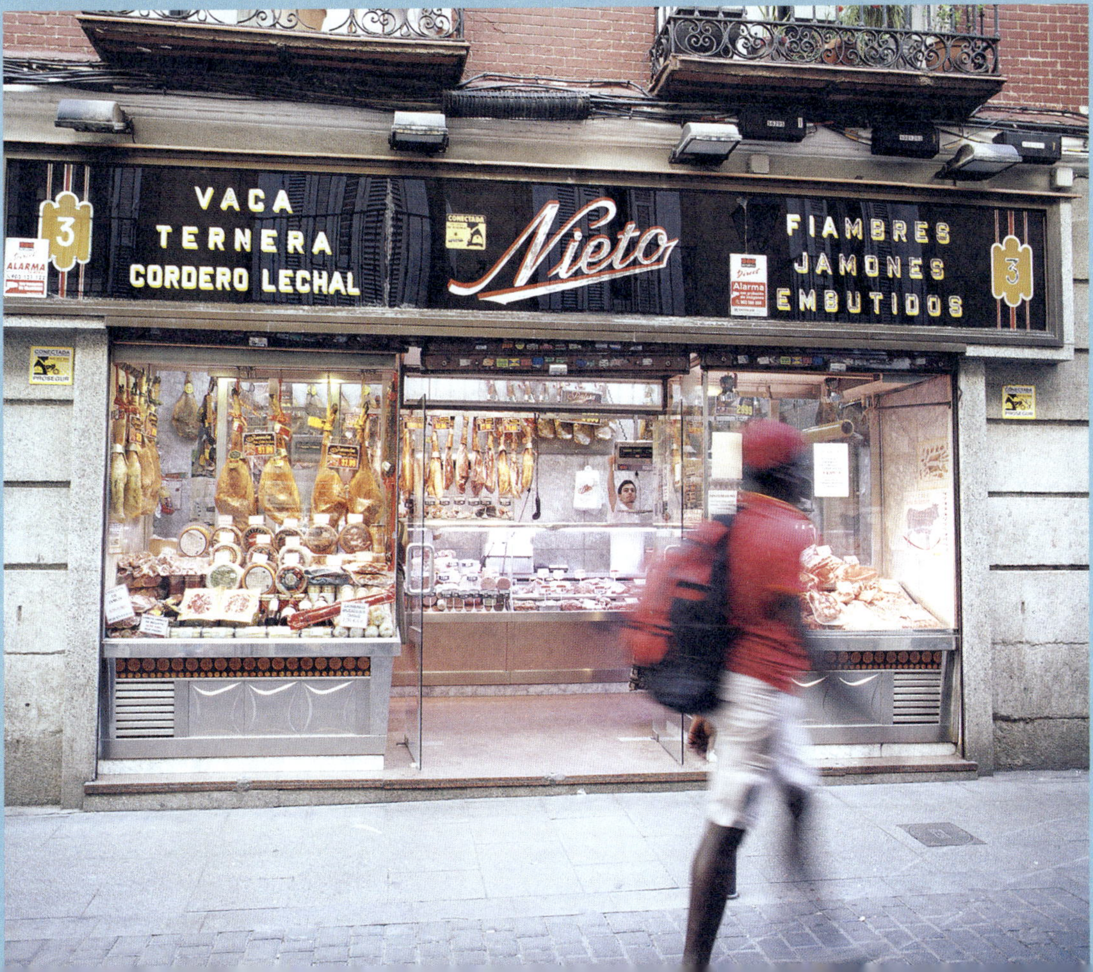
VACA
TERNERA
CORDERO LECHAL
Nieto
FIAMBRES
JAMONES
EMBUTIDOS
3
3
ALARMA

56

Another important thing we took from our time in Naples was about service. Jo's hospo' background was working front of house, and so, service – the style of service – is very important to us. We had a lightbulb moment when we went to lunch one day. Jo's mum was in Naples visiting the family and we found this beautiful restaurant that was cut into the side of a hill overlooking the Bay of Naples. We came to the door and were immediately greeted by a beautiful gentleman in a suit and bow tie who looked at us and said: 'Please, come in.' There was no 'Do you have a booking?' Just 'Come in.'

Everything about the restaurant was about attention to detail. It was there in the crispness of the linen, the way the white-jacketed staff presented themselves, the food, the atmosphere. It all came together to make you feel at ease. It didn't matter if you didn't know exactly what was happening because you just knew that you would be looked after.

We found a similar style of service when we went to Spain. It was in the bars and restaurants, but you'd even find it in the markets too. Vendors would really look at you; they cared about what you wanted to buy and how you were going to cook it. They'd ask you if you wanted your sardines scaled or your fish filleted in a certain way. It's part of the culture to share their talent. It's all part of the service.

We used the markets in Spain as our map. They open out the story for you. You'll be standing behind someone at a stall and there'll be some banter and talk about recipes but also a lot of chat about what's fresh and good that day. It's like the inside scoop of what they'll be eating locally and so, when you head to the tapas bars in the surrounding streets, you have an idea of what to look for.

Sometimes you don't even have to leave the market. There's a market in the Eixample neighbourhood of Barcelona where a lot of the stalls have a bar in them as well. So, the guy selling oysters and shellfish has a little plancha and you can stand in the corner of his shop and have a glass of cava and a freshly shucked oyster or a scallop or some clams off the plancha. Or another guy who stands there and just does anchovies. He gets the anchovy, cleans it, puts it in a marinade and then just serves it up on bread, maybe with some lemon or a little chilli. It's all about using ingredients so good that you can't go wrong.

We based the way we present our specials in Bar Lourinhã on this relationship between the bars and markets that we saw in Spain. We never write our specials down – they're all about having a conversation with our customers so we can explain where and who the ingredients are coming from, why we're serving them and how we're serving them.

It also taps into one of the things we like best about bar dining – the looseness and flexibility of a menu that's driven by what's fresh and available that day. You're in the hands of the chef and the season to an extent, but you can also pick and choose what to eat so you can make your own adventure.

Our first stop in Spain on our fact-finding trip was Valencia. We went there because of how much we liked the market from our last trip. It's a magnificent monument. There's one stall we remembered from our first trip that only sold lemons and garlic. These two ingredients are so central to Matt's cooking and we thought: how could you ever be in the wrong place when it has a shop that just sells lemons and garlic?

From Valencia we had decided to do a circumference of the peninsula, heading along the coast towards Portugal and then circling around from the north and finishing up in Barcelona. We also planned to cross over to Morocco while we were there, to check out the Moorish influence that's so prevalent in a lot of southern Spanish food.

We had some specific things that we wanted to check out. We really wanted to go to Murcia, a town that's slightly inland from the coast that's the home of mojama, the air-dried tuna. Going there was invaluable because it answered some questions that Matt had been having about curing kingfish, and led to the dish that's become a Bar Lourinhã signature: kingfish 'pancetta' with lemon oil (see page 96). The mojama made us realise that texture was as important as flavour and how to get that texture without over-drying, over-curing or over-salting the fish.

Every place we went in Spain we picked up something that we could use. In Cádiz there was a place called Zapata that served grilled meat with an almond sauce. We found a whole series of little kiosk-like bars that served tuna empanadillas and beef empanadillas, which were the inspiration for the rabbit empanadillas that we serve on special occasions at Bar Lourinhã. We washed down amazing prawn pancakes and bacalhau salad with local manzanilla in a seaside town called Sanlúcar de Barrameda.

The biggest influence from Spain on this trip though was Seville. It's a fantastic place: the food, the smells and the Moorish influence in the food and in the architecture. The Middle Eastern influence made us realise we could stretch what we wanted to do. One of the things we were conscious about was not coming back and opening a Spanish bar. We wanted to figure out trying to make it authentically Iberian without saying it was one cuisine or another, which is why we'd always used 'Mediterranean' as our default position. Seville opened up the idea of what Mediterranean food could be, and it made us realise that the parameters of the food we wanted to create were far wider and more adaptable to outside influences than we had ever imagined.

The other thing that happened in Seville that changed the course of the trip – and the way we were thinking about Bar Lourinhã – was the heat. We arrived in Seville during a heatwave with the temperature around 50°C (122°F). Our original itinerary had us heading to Morocco, but the idea of travelling anywhere, let alone travelling south where it was even hotter, was too much to bear; it just wasn't going to happen. We decided to stay in Spain and go to Jerez instead.

It was a great decision. Not only is Jerez home to the best sherry houses in the world, but there's also a really strong bar culture there. We ate a lot of different stuff and came to realise how strong regionality is in Spain. And then we crossed the border into Portugal.

We have Portugal to thank for the name of our bar. All through the trip we were trying to find a name that we liked. We knew it would have the word Bar in the title and so everywhere we went we were looking at names and trying to make them fit: Bar This, Bar That, Something Bar.

One day we were on a bus from Lisbon to Peniche and it stopped in a little rural, working-class town called Lourinhã. It wasn't pretty or particularly unique, just another town. We were sitting on the bus and we said: that's a really beautiful word and it doesn't actually signify anything. It had the Portuguese accent at the end, which we liked, and the town's not well known outside of Portugal so it wouldn't immediately pigeon-hole us into doing one type of food or another. Bar Lourinhã. It just worked.

The name must have had some kind of magic because it was in Portugal that our vision really became clear. We hand-drew a plan of what we wanted our bar to look like (and Bar Lourinhã ended up looking very similar to our very rough sketch) and started to hone specific ideas for dishes that we wanted to serve. We were ready to get home and get going.

MANITAS DE CERDO 3,20
TOMATE 3,15
HUEVO Y MORCILLA BURGOS 3,05
HUEVO Y CHISTORRA 3,05
HUEVO Y CHORIZO 3,05
CHULETÓN GALLEGO
3,00
HUEVO A LA FLAMENCA
NUEVO

The final leg of our trip was in Greece. The other side of Jo's family comes from the island of Samos and she also has cousins in Athens. We had considered this short leg as a time to consolidate what we'd learned on our trip. What we hadn't planned was for Greece to add its influence to Bar Lourinhã too.

From Athens, we took an attitude and approach. Athens is more about street eateries than bars, and you'd often be sitting on the street with the traffic whizzing past while tucking into a plate of sautéed wild greens washed down with a little bottle of ouzo. We loved the sharing style of eating with the mezedes that, instead of being served on single plates like tapas, is served on one big plate with a lot of different stuff. The spaces are relaxed but confident, convivial and open to the elements because of the climate. It's also very seasonal and what you can get to eat in the tavernas is very closely tied to what is available at Athens' main market, which is brilliant, huge, grungy and a bit overwhelming. We love it.

We went to Samos to visit family and to hang out and plan. A passport hiccup meant that Jo had to apply for another passport while we were on the island. It took two and a half months to arrive. And so, Samos, too, found its way into our vision for our own bar in Melbourne.

The bar culture on Samos is all about the beach – they bring the bar and tavern to the beach. Someone will go out fishing that day and then they'll grab some ingredients from the garden and that's what they'll serve in the taverna that night. And you get something to eat the moment you sit down. They do this in Spain, Italy and Portugal as well and it was something we wanted to do when we opened Bar Lourinhã. From day one, we had a five-minute rule in the kitchen – when someone comes in and sits down, we don't want them waiting any longer than five minutes for their first snack. It could be just a bowl of olives but we wanted to carry that attitude through – welcome, come in, here's something to eat, let us look after you.

The thing that we really loved about Samos was the freshness of the ingredients. In Spain, there is a lot more fried food than there is in Greece and Italy. We didn't want a big fryer in the kitchen and so we looked at the bar food in Greece and Italy. We combined those influences – stuff off the grill, stuff that is raw – and melded them with the Spanish idea of something small and bitey and freshly made.

We were on Samos when we found the right premises for Bar Lourinhã. It had the right amount of space, the right location and it would easily fit the design that we had in our head.

It was a fast turnaround, like Bar Lourinhã was eager to be born. We returned to Australia in December, had the keys to the building in February and served our first customer in May. The budget was tiny, so we had to do a lot of the work ourselves. The joinery was built offsite from recycled jarrah by our mate Nick Coyle, the refrigeration and cooking equipment was all second-hand and we decorated the place with second-hand stuff – an old Ricon sign, an old mirror, copper pots and religious paraphernalia from Jo's grandmother. Jo's photos were also a big part of the décor and we magnet-pinned them to the walls because we couldn't afford to get them framed.

We couldn't even think about the upstairs space we had in those early days, but that was OK because, at the end of the day, the heart and soul of the business was always going to be the bar, both upstairs and down.

The design of our first menu was inspired by a tapas bar in Seville. It was clear, concise and it made it easy to understand what we were serving. That was important to us because what we were trying to do at Bar Lourinhã was to educate people in a different style of dining, a different philosophy and attitude. We figured it was part of our job to guide them through.

What we hadn't factored into the equation was that Australians are adventurous diners. They took to the food almost straight away. The service technique and style took a little longer to get across but as soon as people got used to it and realised that the service was fine-dining standard but in a looser format, they embraced it.

We had our first 'oh my god we've done it right' moment in the first week. There were about 10 to 15 people sitting at the bar at lunchtime, everybody happy and everybody eating exactly like you would eat in Spain. And it was like: they get it! All the research and travel, all the eating and drinking in bars, all the talking to people about ingredients and observing how they looked after people came together at that moment. All the thinking about what it was about bars that we loved so much. It was early days and a really small thing, but it reassured us that we were on the right track. Two decades later, we're still going strong. Seems like people really did want to eat at the bar.

As Bar Lourinhã turns 20, we're appreciating what we've created, and the special community that has come with it. And we're looking forward to the future, with more good times, travels and adventures.

OCEAN
MADE
SEAFOOD

EXIT

RINCÓN Del 2x4

Tapas

Tapas, antipasti, mezze, snacks. Regardless of their label or origin, we have always been drawn towards little bits (and big bits) of food that go well with a good drink. We love that you can create something really punchy in just one bite. We never wanted Bar Lourinhã to be a tapas bar, but found grazing on small snacks a great way to eat or begin a big meal. This selection of tapas includes some of our most revered customer favourites, and a mixture of these dishes makes the perfect start to a dinner party at home – or they can even be enjoyed as a main course.

Oysters

The best oysters we've ever eaten come from the north-west corner of Spain. In this little town called Vigo, in Galicia, there was this one street full of bars where all these old women dressed in traditional white aprons were shucking oysters in the street. They store their oysters in commercial fridges set up on the street by the council. Then the women come into the bars and sell the shucked oysters. They'd roll their eyes if you only ordered a dozen, so we usually ended up tucking into 24 oysters at a time. We've always served oysters at Bar Lourinhã in a similar way – as fresh as we can get them, shucked to order and served with nothing but a squeeze of lemon.

King Prawn & Pork Pincho

MAKES 12

Pinchos are the perfect tapas dish. In Madrid, they get the pincho, stick it in a roll and then pull the skewer out so everything's contained in the roll and you eat it like a bocadillo.

- 12 cooked king prawns (shrimp), heads and shells removed
- 100 ml (3½ fl oz) Chilli Oil (page 173), plus extra to serve
- 100 g (3½ oz) chicharrón (fried pork skin), crushed
- 50 g (1¾ oz/½ cup) dry breadcrumbs
- salt and freshly ground black pepper

Insert either a metal or wooden skewer into the tail of each prawn, pushing all the way through to the head as straight as possible. Using a pastry brush, baste the prawns with the chilli oil.

Mix together the chicharrón, breadcrumbs and some salt and pepper in a small baking tray. One at a time, dredge the prawns in the crumb mix until evenly coated. Serve on a platter with a little extra chilli oil.

{Pictured on page 27}

MANZANILLA

The seaside town of Sanlúcar de Barrameda is home to this delicious salty and dry aperitif sherry. Served icy cold, it matches perfectly with King Prawn & Pork Pinchos or Prawn Croquetas.

Prawn Croquetas

MAKES 25–30

This is one of our favourites, not just because it's our biggest selling item at the bar, but because these little beauties ooze all the goodness of what a croqueta can be. We love the mix of the two different textures – the creamy texture of the béchamel and the firm texture of the prawn pieces – plus the way the prawn flavour infuses into everything else.

1 litre (34 fl oz/4 cups) full-cream (whole) milk

2 garlic cloves, smashed

2 bay leaves

3 prawn (shrimp) heads (optional)

salt and freshly ground black pepper

200 g (7 oz) butter, diced

225 g (8 oz/1½ cups) plain (all-purpose) flour

250 g (9 oz/2 cups) prawns (shrimp), cooked, peeled and roughly chopped

blended olive oil, for deep-frying

sea salt, to serve

Aioli, to serve (page 164)

CRUMB

450 g (1 lb/3 cups) plain (all-purpose) flour seasoned with salt and pepper

4 free-range eggs and 125 ml (4 fl oz/½ cup) full-cream (whole) milk, whisked

250 g (9 oz/2½ cups) fine dry breadcrumbs

Place the milk, garlic, bay leaves and prawn heads (if using) in a large saucepan and season with salt and pepper. Bring to the boil. As soon as it boils, turn the heat off and leave to steep for 5 minutes then strain through a fine-mesh sieve into a jug, discarding the solids.

In another saucepan, gently melt the butter over a medium heat, then add the flour. Stir well and cook for about 5 minutes, until the flour is cooked through. Carefully add the strained milk in a slow but steady stream, whisking continuously to avoid lumps.

Continue cooking the croqueta mixture for another 10 minutes until quite smooth and thick. Remove from the heat and add the prawns, stirring well to make sure they are evenly combined. Pour the mixture into a baking tray and transfer to the fridge to cool.

Once cool, use a spoon to measure out 50 g (1¾ oz) scoops until all the mixture has been used, then squeeze and roll each scoop to form a log shape roughly 6–8 cm (2½–3¼ in) long. For the crumbs, dip each log first in the seasoned flour, then in the egg mixture, then roll in the breadcrumbs.

Heat enough oil for deep-frying in a large, heavy-based saucepan or deep-fryer until the oil reaches 160°C (320°F) on a cooking thermometer. Fry about 6–8 croquetas at a time, then drain on paper towels and serve, still piping hot, with a good pinch of sea salt and a side of aioli.

{ Pictured on page 30 }

PRAWN CROQUETAS

BOLINHOS DE BACALHAU

FRIED QUESO FRESCO, CAPER & GUINDILLA CHILLI

Bolinhos de Bacalhau

MAKES 25–30

This is Jo's favourite, she's always bugging me to make them. We use whole bacalhau with skin and bones, then soak them and preserve the cooking water to cook the potatoes so we get some of that salty fishy goodness. The first time we had bolinhos de bacalhau was in Lisbon. They made them with big chunks of fish and potato and it was like having a gooey fried fish-and-chip ball. Awesome. We add parsley and lemon to our recipe, just to give it a kick of flavour and freshness.

300 g (10½ oz) bacalhau (salt cod), soaked overnight in water and refreshed at least three times

3 garlic cloves (2 left whole, 1 crushed)

2 dried bay leaves

1 kg (2 lb 3 oz) Desiree potatoes, peeled

grated zest of 2 lemons

1 free-range egg

15 g (½ oz/½ cup) chopped flat-leaf (Italian) parsley

salt and freshly ground black pepper

185 g (6½ oz/1¼ cups) plain (all-purpose) flour, sifted

blended vegetable oil, for deep-frying

Aioli, to serve (page 164)

Drain the bacalhau and place it in a large saucepan with 3 litres (101 fl oz/12 cups) cold water, the whole garlic cloves and bay leaves. Bring to the boil and simmer for 5 minutes. Turn the heat off and leave to sit for another 5 minutes. Transfer the bacalhau to a tray and cool in the refrigerator. Reserve the cooking water for the potatoes. When the bacalhau is cool enough to touch, remove all the bones and gently mash the flesh with a fork.

Place the potatoes in the reserved cooking water and bring to the boil. Simmer until the potatoes are cooked through. Drain well, discard the bay leaves and garlic cloves and ensure the potatoes are dry before mashing. Pass the potatoes through a mouli or potato ricer and mash into a large mixing bowl.½

Add the bacalhau, lemon zest, egg, parsley, crushed garlic and salt and pepper to taste, then mix well. Form a well in the mixture and scatter the flour over the potato mixture. Working very gently, use the back of a wooden spoon to mix until just combined. Measure the mixture into 50 g (1¾ oz) pieces and roll into balls with your hands or shape into quenelles using two dessert spoons.

Heat enough oil for deep-frying in a large, heavy-based saucepan or deep-fryer until the oil reaches 160°C (320°F) on a cooking thermometer. Fry 8–10 bolinhos at a time until golden and crunchy. Serve hot with the aioli.

{ Pictured on page 30 }

Fried Queso Fresco, Caper & Guindilla Chilli

MAKES 25–30

This is a riff on a Sicilian fresh cheese fritter that we've mixed with guindilla chillies, the classic pickled green chillies of Spain. It's a great vegetarian option for a fried tapa, super simple and delivers a good hit of salt from the caper and a tingle of heat from the chilli.

1 kg (2 lb 3 oz) queso fresco, or ricotta

1 free-range egg

120 g (4½ oz/1 cup) chopped guindilla chilli

50 g (1¾ oz/⅓ cup) baby vinegared capers

grated zest of 1 lemon

2 garlic cloves, crushed

pinch of salt, plus extra to serve

1 teaspoon cracked black pepper

150 g (5½ oz/1 cup) self-raising flour, sifted

blended olive oil, for deep-frying

sea salt, to serve

Green Chilli Aioli, to serve (page 165)

Combine all the ingredients except the flour and oil in a bowl and mix thoroughly. Form a well in the middle and scatter the flour over the cheese. Using the back of a wooden spoon, gently mix the flour into the cheese until just combined.

Measure out 50 g (1¾ oz) scoops of the mixture and roll each into a perfect ball. Refrigerate until ready to cook.

Add enough oil for deep-frying to a large, heavy-based saucepan or deep-fryer and heat the oil until it reaches 160°C (320°F) on a cooking thermometer. Fry about 6–8 fritti at a time until lightly golden, then drain on paper towels.

Arrange the balls on a plate, sprinkle with some sea salt and serve with the green chilli aioli.

{ Pictured on page 31 }

Mr Monaco

30 ml (1 fl oz) Melbourne Gin Company gin

30 ml (1 fl oz) Aperol

15 ml (½ fl oz) lemon juice

15 ml (½ fl oz) Sugar Syrup (page 176)

1 egg white

ice cubes, for shaking

Peychaud's bitters, to garnish

This cocktail was named after the Honorary Consul-General of Monaco (Bar Lourinhã's neighbour in Little Collins Street, Melbourne), who became so entranced by its sweet and sour fluffiness that he claimed it as the perfect alternative to a protein shake.

Combine all the ingredients except the ice in a shaker and shake vigorously for 10 seconds. Top with ice and shake well again. Strain into a cocktail glass and garnish with a spray or a few drops of bitters.

Tinto de Verano

60 ml (2 fl oz/¼ cup) Liquor 43

60 ml (2 fl oz/¼ cup) freshly squeezed lemon juice

½ orange, cut into 5 wedges

15 mint leaves, torn

360 ml (12 fl oz) rosé

ice cubes, to serve

lemonade, to serve

We first tasted this drink on a very hot night in Seville. We had discovered one of the coolest bars in the Macarena district and saw everyone drinking this light, refreshing red wine spritzer. We tweaked it by using rosé instead of red wine and it's now our go-to for customers asking for sangria.

Build all the ingredients in a large glass serving jug. Top with ice and fill up with lemonade. Stir well before serving.

SPIRITS

The cocktail philosophy at Bar Lourinhã is to use the finest base spirits. When we travel, we look out for rare and classic spirits, which seem to make their way back to Australia in our suitcase.

DON JOSÉ

Stolen Town Bike

30 ml (1 fl oz) vodka

30 ml (1 fl oz) Oloroso

10 ml (¼ fl oz) Sugar Syrup (page 176)

1 dash grapefruit bitters

45 ml (1½ fl oz) freshly squeezed grapefruit juice

ice cubes, for shaking

grapefruit soda, to serve

grapefruit twist, to garnish

Combine all the ingredients in a cocktail shaker and top with ice, then shake vigorously for about 10 seconds. Strain into a highball glass, top up with grapefruit soda and garnish with a grapefruit twist.

Chorizo Croquetas

MAKES 25–30

We do three different types of croqueta – classic béchamel, a Portuguese-style potato version and then cheese-based ones. This one is a potato croqueta. They can be tricky to make if the potato isn't right. It has to have the right starch and sugar levels because if those are out of balance they'll be too gooey and can discolour. You need to make sure the potatoes are in season (they're best in autumn) and use varieties like Dutch Cream or Desiree – potatoes with yellow flesh rather than white. Get the potato right and it's quite simple.

- 1 kg (2 lb 3 oz) Desiree potatoes, peeled
- 1 free-range egg
- 300 g (10½ oz/1½ cups) dried chorizo, skin removed and finely diced (see Note)
- 2 garlic cloves, crushed
- salt and freshly ground black pepper
- 150 g (5½ oz/1 cup) plain (all-purpose) flour, sifted
- blended olive oil, for deep-frying
- Pimentón Salt, to serve (page 172)
- Aioli, to serve (page 164)

Put the potatoes in a large saucepan and cover with cold water. Add a large pinch of salt and bring to the boil. Continue boiling until the potatoes are just beginning to soften. Drain well, then pass the potatoes through a mouli or potato ricer on a coarse setting into a large mixing bowl.

Allow the potato to cool slightly before adding the egg, chorizo, garlic and some salt and pepper. Mix well. Add the flour and gently mix until only just combined. Measure the mixture into 50 g (1¾ oz) pieces and roll into balls between floured hands or shape into quenelles using two dessert spoons.

Heat enough oil for deep-frying in a large, heavy-based saucepan or deep-fryer until it reaches 170°C (340°F) on a cooking thermometer. Fry the croquetas in small batches. Serve piping hot with a generous sprinkling of pimentón salt on a generous dollop of aioli.

Note Ideally a longaniça or semi curado–style chorizo would be perfect. Choose a spicy one if you prefer.

Jamón Croquetas

MAKES 25–30

You see more jamón croquetas in Spain than any other type. In a lot of markets and delis you'd see mixed bowls of offcuts and rinds from cured meats. People buy them to use in different types of soups, and chop them up and put them into a béchamel sauce to make croquetas. The older the meat gets, the more intense the flavour.

- 1 litre (34 fl oz/4 cups) full-cream (whole) milk
- 2 garlic cloves, smashed
- 2 dried bay leaves
- salt and freshly ground black pepper
- 200 g (7 oz) butter, diced
- 225 g (8 oz/1½ cups)
- plain (all-purpose) flour
- 100 g (3½ oz/2 cups) jamón offcuts, finely diced
- blended olive oil, for deep-frying
- sea salt, to serve
- Aioli, to serve (page 164)

CRUMB

- 450 g (1 lb/3 cups) plain (all-purpose) flour seasoned with salt and pepper
- 4 free-range eggs and 125 ml (4 fl oz/½ cup) full-cream (whole) milk, whisked
- 250 g (9 oz/2½ cups) fine dry breadcrumbs

Combine the milk, garlic, bay leaves and some salt and pepper in a saucepan and bring to the boil. As soon as it boils, turn the heat off and leave to steep for 5 minutes, then strain through a fine-mesh sieve into a jug, discarding the solids.

In another saucepan, gently melt the butter over a medium heat then add the flour. Stir well to form a roux and cook the flour out for about 5 minutes over a medium–high heat. In a slow but steady stream, add the strained milk to the roux, whisking continuously to avoid lumps. Continue cooking the croqueta mixture for another 10 minutes until quite smooth and thick. Remove from the heat and add the diced jamón, stirring until evenly combined. Pour into a baking tray and transfer to the fridge to cool.

Once cool, measure the mixture into 50 g (1¾ oz) pieces, then squeeze and roll each piece into a log shape roughly 6–8 cm (2½–3¼ in) long. For the crumbs, dip each log first in the seasoned flour, then in the egg mixture, then roll in the breadcrumbs.

Heat enough oil for deep-frying in a large, heavy-based saucepan or deep-fryer until the oil reaches 160°C (320°F) on a cooking thermometer. Fry about 6–8 croquetas at a time, then drain on paper towels. Serve hot with a good pinch of sea salt and a side of aioli.

Sardine Bocadillos

MAKES 8

We've always been fans of the fish sandwich that you find all through the Mediterranean, and we thought it would be a really good fit at Bar Lourinhã. We get beautiful fresh sardines from Lakes Entrance in Victoria's north-east.

- 8 sardine fillets
- freshly ground black pepper, to taste
- 1 tablespoon olive oil
- 8 mini hot dog or brioche buns
- 4 tablespoons Lemon Aioli (page 166)
- 8 sorrel leaves
- 8 guindilla chillies, each cut into three pieces
- 10 g (1/4 oz/ 1/3 cup) flat-leaf (Italian) parsley leaves
- 1 teaspoon pink peppercorns, crushed, to serve
- 1 teaspoon Chilli Salt, to serve (page 172)

Season the sardines with black pepper. Heat the oil in a frying pan over a medium heat and fry the sardines, skin side down, for 2 minutes, then remove from the heat and allow to cool.

Slice the buns in half and spread both halves with lemon aioli, then place a sorrel leaf inside each bun. Put the cooked sardine fillet on top of the sorrel, then top with the chilli and parsley leaves. To serve, season with pink peppercorns and chilli salt and cover with the top bun.

Morcilla Croquetas, Salsa Picante

MAKES 25–30

Blood sausage is one of those things that we've always had at Bar Lourinhã, either bought or ones we've done in-house. It's everywhere in the south of Spain but it always surprised us how many people go for the morcilla at our place. Blood is a great seller, especially when it's spicy and mixed with potato. It takes you to the south of Spain immediately.

- 1 kg (2 lb 3 oz) Desiree potatoes, peeled
- 1 free-range egg
- 200 g (7 oz/2 cups) morcilla (blood sausage), finely diced
- 1 tablespoon pimentón
- salt and freshly ground black pepper
- 150 g (5½ oz/1 cup) plain (all-purpose) flour, sifted
- blended olive oil, for deep-frying
- Pimentón Salt, to serve (page 172)
- Salsa Picante, to serve (page 162)

Put the potatoes in a large saucepan and cover with cold water. Add a large pinch of salt and bring to the boil. Keep at a steady boil until the potatoes are just beginning to soften. Drain well, then pass the potatoes through a mouli or potato ricer on a coarse setting into a large mixing bowl.

Add the egg, morcilla, pimentón and salt and pepper to taste. Mix well.

Add the flour and gently mix until only just combined. Measure the mixture into 50 g (1¾ oz) pieces and roll into balls between floured hands.

Add enough oil for deep-frying to a large, heavy-based saucepan or deep-fryer and heat the oil until it reaches 160°C (320°F) on a cooking thermometer. Fry about 6–8 croquetas at a time, then drain on paper towels. Serve piping hot with a generous sprinkling of the pimentón salt on a generous dollop of salsa picante.

Smoked Eel Croquetas

MAKES 25-30

Smoked eel became a thing in Melbourne because there are great producers in the surrounding regions and Matt worked with a lot of eel during his apprenticeship. It's a great-tasting product, fatty and rich and pretty easy to get. We hadn't eaten a smoked eel croqueta anywhere before, so I guess this is a Bar Lourinhã original.

750 ml (25½ fl oz/3 cups) full-cream (whole) milk

250 ml (8½ fl oz/1 cup) fish stock

2 garlic cloves, smashed

2 dried bay leaves

salt and freshly ground black pepper

200 g (7 oz) butter, diced

225 g (8 oz/1½ cups) plain (all-purpose) flour

400 g (14 oz/3 cups) smoked eel (skin and bones removed), finely chopped

15 g (½ oz/½ cup) chopped flat-leaf (Italian) parsley

blended olive oil, for deep-frying

Aioli, to serve (page 166)

CRUMB

250 g (9 oz/2½ cups) fine dry breadcrumbs

grated zest of 2 lemons

450 g (1 lb/3 cups) plain (all-purpose) flour seasoned with salt and pepper

4 free-range eggs and 125 ml (4 fl oz/½ cup) full-cream (whole) milk, whisked

Combine the milk, stock, garlic, bay leaves and some salt and pepper in a large saucepan and bring to the boil. As soon as it boils, turn the heat off and leave to steep for 5 minutes, then strain into a jug, discarding the solids.

In another saucepan, gently melt the butter over a medium heat then add the flour. Stir well to form a roux and cook the flour out for about 5 minutes over a medium–high heat. In a slow but steady stream, add the strained milk to the roux, whisking continuously to avoid lumps. Continue cooking the croqueta mixture for another 10 minutes, stirring continuously with a spoon, until it is quite smooth and thick. Remove from the heat and add the eel and parsley, stirring until evenly combined. Pour into a baking tray and transfer to the fridge to cool.

Once cool, measure the mixture into 40 g (1½ oz) pieces, then squeeze and roll each piece into a log shape roughly 5 cm (2 in) long. For the crumbs, mix the breadcrumbs and lemon zest together. Dip each log first in the seasoned flour, then in the egg mixture, then roll in the breadcrumbs.

Add enough oil for deep-frying to a large, heavy-based saucepan or deep-fryer and heat the oil until it reaches 160°C (320°F) on a cooking thermometer. Fry until they are lightly brown and floating, then drain on paper towels. Serve piping hot with a good pinch of sea salt and a side of aioli.

Pickled Sardine Banderillas

MAKES 12

Banderillas are always in cabinets in the bars in Spain and they're a lot of fun because you can put anything you like on a stick. They're quick and easy to eat too, which means you can have more of them. Banderillas are tiny replicas of the weapons used in bull fighting (also called banderillas), which is both distressing and romantically nostalgic.

- 6 sardine fillets, halved lengthways
- juice of 2 lemons
- 2 tablespoons olive oil, plus extra for drizzling
- salt and freshly ground black pepper
- 6 guindilla chillies (halved lengthways if large)
- 12 small pickled onions
- 12 flat-leaf (Italian) parsley leaves
- 12 cornichons

Put the sardine fillets in a bowl and add the lemon juice, olive oil and some salt and pepper. Mix gently and allow to stand for 1 hour before assembling the banderillas.

Start by threading the guindillas onto twelve 12 cm (4¾ in) decorative serving sticks. Next, add the onions, parsley leaves and rolled sardine fillets, then finish with the cornichons. Arrange on a serving plate with a drizzle of olive oil and some freshly ground pepper.

Octopus Banderillas

MAKES 12

We like to use fresh herbs on our banderillas because they help to cut through some of the vinegar. The octopus we use here is the tentacles from our Greek octopus recipe (see page 124). Instead of putting it on the grill, we just put the cold steamed octopus straight onto the stick and finish it with a good slug of olive oil.

- 12 guindilla chillies
- 12 flat-leaf (Italian) parsley leaves
- 3 piquillo peppers, cut into 12 pieces
- 1 cooked octopus tentacle, cut into 12 slices (see page 124)
- 12 thick cucumber slices
- olive oil, for drizzling
- freshly ground black pepper

Assemble the banderillas by threading the guindillas onto 12 cm (4¾ in) decorative serving sticks. Place the parsley leaves on the piquillo peppers, roll up and thread onto the sticks. Add a piece of octopus and finish with the cucumber. Arrange on a serving plate with a drizzle of olive oil and some freshly ground pepper.

Chilli-pickled Cucumbers

SERVES 4

Often when we were returning from Europe to Australia we would stop off somewhere in Asia for a week or so. This recipe was inspired by those trips – it's super crunchy, crisp and really refreshing, great for the warmer months when cucumbers are at their peak.

- 60 ml (2 fl oz/¼ cup) sweet white-wine vinegar
- 2 tablespoons Salsa Picante (page 162)
- 1 teaspoon chilli flakes
- ½ teaspoon salt
- 1 teaspoon caster (superfine) sugar
- ¼ teaspoon freshly ground black pepper
- 2 shallots, finely sliced
- 500 g (1 lb 2 oz) Lebanese (short) cucumbers, sliced into long fingers
- 2 tablespoons freshly chopped dill

Combine all the ingredients except the cucumbers and dill in a bowl. Mix well, then add the cucumbers, mix again, and refrigerate for at least 2 hours before serving. Top with freshly chopped dill.

TIP

Used as a garnish for cocktails, these pickles can lend a spicy, savoury twist to old favourites, such as a bloody Mary or even a classic martini garnished with a pickled guindilla chilli.

Crispy Zucchini Flowers & Stretched Curd

MAKES 12

This is a tribute to Jo's grandmother Lidia. When Matt was trying to work out this cooking thing, spending time with her in her backyard in Box Hill (a tiny patch of land that produced an enormous amount of food) really started to define how he wanted to go about it. There are great old photos of Matt picking zucchini flowers with Lidia. We've refined the batter slightly to make it silky, but the filling is exactly as Lidia would have done it.

12 zucchini (courgette) flowers (male or female are fine)

1 fior di latte, cut into 12 cubes (see Note)

blended olive oil, for deep-frying

sea salt flakes, to serve

Aioli, to serve (page 164)

BATTER

75 g (2¾ oz/½ cup) self-raising flour

250 ml (8½ fl oz/1 cup) soda water (club soda)

To make the batter, put the flour in a mixing bowl and form a well in the middle. Pour in the soda water and whisk briskly to combine. The batter should be the consistency of thick cream. Refrigerate until needed.

To stuff the flowers, gently tear one side of the flower open. Place a cube of cheese inside and seal it shut.

Add enough oil for deep-frying to a large, heavy-based saucepan or deep-fryer and heat the oil until it reaches 160°C (320°F) on a cooking thermometer. Working one at a time, dip each flower in the batter and coat well. Using your fingers, gently wipe off a little excess batter by stroking the flower from the tip to the bottom of the stem. Fry the flowers quickly until lightly golden, then drain on paper towels and serve warm with a sprinkling of sea salt and a side of aioli.

Note Fior di latte is a fresh-style mozzarella the size of a baseball. You can substitute it for bocconcini.

{Pictured on page 47}

House Pickles

MAKES 2 LITRES (68 FL OZ/ 8 CUPS)

A lot of bars in Granada give away free tapas and sometimes it'll just be a bowl of pickled vegetables, which might sound boring but is actually a great way to start off having a nibble and a drink. They use a highly acidic vinegar and a lot of salt and it's great with the crunch of the vegetables. It became a thing when we were writing the menu at Bar Lourinhã – there were always pickles and nuts to start with. Use any form of in-season hard veg and do them in large quantities because they store really well.

1 cauliflower, cut into small florets (see Note)

3 firm green tomatoes, cut into 5 mm (1/4 in) slices

15 g (1/2 oz/1/2 cup) coriander (cilantro) leaves

PICKLING LIQUOR

1 litre (34 fl oz/4 cups) white vinegar

250 ml (8 1/2 fl oz/1 cup) dry white wine

1/2 tablespoon salt

1/2 tablespoon caster (superfine) sugar

1 cinnamon stick

1 star anise

2 garlic cloves, peeled

2 fresh bay leaves

1 teaspoon whole black peppercorns

2 teaspoons brown mustard seeds

For the pickling liquor, combine all the ingredients in a saucepan and bring to the boil. Taste and adjust the seasoning to ensure an evenness between sweet, sour and salty. Add the cauliflower and simmer over a low heat for 4 minutes. Remove from the heat and leave to cool inthe liquid.

Once the pickling liquor is completely cool, add the tomatoes and coriander leaves. Transfer the pickles to a sterilised glass jar (see below), seal with a lid and leave it in a cool, dark place for 4 days. Store in the refrigerator for up to 6 months.

Note The vegetables for our pickles vary from season to season. Use this pickling liquor to pickle a whole range of pickled vegetables. Just remember to adjust the cooking times as needed. The vegetables should still be crisp, but just starting to soften.

Sterilising glass To keep your dishes tasting fresh and free of any contaminants, it's important to sterilise any glass bottles or jars before use. Thoroughly wash the bottles and lids in hot soapy water. Place on a baking tray, mouths facing up, and leave in a very low oven until completely dry.

Spritz de Portugal

- 45 ml (1½ fl oz) white port
- juice of ¼ lemon
- ice cubes, to serve
- cava, to serve
- guindilla chilli and lemon slice, to garnish

Build the white port and lemon juice in a wine glass, then top with ice. Top up with cava and garnish with a guindilla chilli and a slice of lemon to serve.

CAVA

The Spanish equivalent to prosecco, cava is produced predominantly in Catalonia. We love the freshness, vibrant bubbles and brut dryness. Perfect to drink on its own or to jazz up in a spritz.

Anchovy 'Montadito'

MAKES 12

We've always used anchovies from Cantabria on the Atlantic coast. They're caught, filleted and salted straight away. A lot of the really good ones are hand-filleted, so it's a pretty intensive process and the prices reflect that. But I would challenge anyone to find an anchovy outside of that region that comes anywhere close. Don't skimp for this recipe – it's so simple, but it relies on you using a remarkable anchovy.

- ⅔ loaf square sourdough, preferably at least 1 day old
- 100 ml (3½ fl oz) Garlic Oil (see Note)
- 5 g (⅛ oz) fine salt
- 12 fine anchovy fillets, preferably Spanish
- 1 tablespoon olive oil
- 1 tablespoon thyme leaves, to garnish

Using a sharp knife, remove the crusts from the loaf and slice the bread into soldiers, about 10 × 1 cm (4 × ½ in). Douse the bread in the garlic oil and salt and place on a hot grill or in a hot chargrill pan. Grill all four sides until evenly charred, then transfer to a serving plate.

Using a sharp knife, make an incision down the length of the bread fingers – being sure not to cut all the way through – and insert an anchovy fillet in each slit. Finish with a splash of olive oil and garnish with thyme leaves.

Note Garlic oil is simple to make, just add 1 crushed garlic clove to 100 ml (3½ fl oz) olive oil.

Lardo

MAKES 1 KG (2 LB 3 OZ)

This recipe was developed over time using a combination of methods. I highly recommend reading one of the many books specialising in cured meats prior to attempting this recipe.

3 kg (6 lb 10 oz) coarse rock salt

250 g (9 oz) fine salt

8 dried bay leaves

½ bunch thyme sprigs

15 whole black peppercorns, lightly bruised

1 kg (2 lb 3 oz) slab pork back fat

Mix together the salts, bay leaves, thyme and peppercorns in a bowl until well combined.

In a non-reactive/plastic container, add a thin base layer of salt and place the pork fat on top. Scatter the remaining salt over the meat and rub it in to the top of the fat. Place a lid on top and transfer the container to the fridge for roughly 3–4 weeks.

Check the salt regularly for signs of moisture; the mixture should remain quite dry for the entire process. If it is too moist, scrape the existing salt off the meat and replace with a fresh batch of salt.

The lardo is ready when it has lost its brilliant white colour and firms up slightly. Wrap the lardo tightly in plastic wrap and store it for use in the refrigerator for 6–9 months.

Lardo Soldiers

MAKES 12

This recipe is based on a dish we had in Barcelona at a bar called El Xampanyet. We went in because we saw an old guy working behind the bar. In Spain now a lot of bars are made to look old so it's sometimes tricky to tell if they're a chain or if they've been there for 50 years. Hot tip: a chain won't hire someone who's 70 years old to work behind the bar. We ordered a plate of picos wrapped in beautiful pale-pink lardo and have been hooked ever since. The Bar Lourinhã version is slightly different: warm toasted bread instead of picos so the lardo melts into it. It's one of those snacks where people order a second plate before they've finished the first.

- ⅔ loaf square sourdough, preferably at least 1 day old
- 100 ml (3½ fl oz) Garlic Oil (page 52)
- 5 g (⅛ oz) fine salt
- 12 slices Lardo, sliced very thin (page 54)
- Chilli Salt, to serve (page 172)
- ½ tablespoon lemon thyme leaves, to serve
- olive oil, for drizzling

Using a sharp knife, remove the crusts from the loaf and slice the bread into soldiers, about 2 cm (¾ in) square.

Douse the bread in the garlic oil and salt and place on a hot grill or in a hot chargrill pan. Grill all four sides until evenly charred, then remove from the grill and immediately wrap the soldiers in the lardo.

Place on a serving plate and sprinkle over the chilli salt, thyme leaves and a heavy drizzle of olive oil.

Morcilla Cigar & Smoked Chilli

MAKES 20

We use brik pastry here, which is outside the box in terms of where we've travelled, but it's something that Matt's used throughout his career. It's a really beautiful pastry because it gets an amazing crispness on it so quickly. This is such a simple recipe: just morcilla cut into cubed fingers, an egg wash and a super-quick fry so you end up with a translucent pastry with gooey sausage inside and a bit of dried, smoked chipotle on top. You can eat a lot of them.

3 morcilla sausages

4 brik pastry sheets, cut into 8-cm (3¼-in) squares

free-range egg white

olive oil, for deep-frying

Smoked Chilli Aioli, to serve (page 165)

Chipotle Salt, to serve (page 172)

Slice the morcilla into cubed fingers about 1 cm (½ in) wide and roughly 8 cm (3¼ in) long.

Place the sausage fingers on the brik pastry, then lightly brush with egg white and roll up tightly. Pack the 'cigars' in a sealed container and refrigerate until ready to cook.

Add enough oil for deep-frying to a large, heavy-based saucepan or deep-fryer and heat the oil until it reaches 160°C (320°F) on a cooking thermometer. Fry a few cigars at a time until golden and crispy, then remove and drain on paper towels. Serve the cigars on a base of smoked chilli aioli and sprinkle with chipotle salt.

Pig's Head, Mojo Picon & Fried Bread

MAKES 30

The fried bread component here is loosely inspired by the Catalan flatbread, coca. Fried bread slathered with lots of punchy stuff is never a bad idea. We ate a few versions of it in Barcelona on our last trip. Mojo picon is a paprika-based sauce with chilli in it and goes beautifully with the fatty pig's head. It has loads and loads of flavour. It's best to eat the bread hot, straight out of the fryer.

Mojo Picon, to serve (page 169)

fennel fronds, to garnish

FRIED BREAD

12 g (¼ oz) dried yeast

1 teaspoon honey

3 tablespoons olive oil

pinch of salt

620 g (1 lb 6 oz) plain (all-purpose) flour, plus extra for dusting

PIG'S HEAD

1 small pig's head

2 carrots, roughly chopped

1 celery stalk, roughly chopped

2 onions, roughly chopped

2 tablespoons ground (chipotle) chilli

2 tablespoons Garlic Oil (page 52)

salt and freshly ground black pepper

To make the fried bread, combine the yeast with 400 ml (13½ fl oz) warm water, the honey and oil in a bowl. Leave in a warm part of the kitchen for about 15 minutes until the yeast activates and the mixture begins to bubble.

Mix the salt and flour in the bowl of a stand mixer fitted with the dough hook attachment. Slowly pour in the activated yeast water and continue mixing on low speed for 10 minutes. Cover the bowl of the mixer with plastic wrap and leave the dough to prove for 1 hour, or until doubled in size. Cut the dough into 15 g (½ oz) pieces and roll into balls. Refrigerate until ready to serve.

For the pig's head, place the head in a large saucepan and cover with salted water. Add the carrots, celery and onion and bring to the boil. Reduce the heat and simmer for around 2½ hours, or until the meat is falling off the bone. Remove from the heat and allow to cool, then, using gloves, remove all the meat from the head and chop it into small pieces. Place in a mixing bowl and season generously with the ground chipotle, garlic oil and salt and pepper to taste.

To assemble, stretch each ball of dough into a small raft shape. Add enough oil for deep-frying to a large, heavy-based saucepan or deep-fryer and heat the oil until it reaches 160°C (320°F) on a cooking thermometer. Fry the bread until lightly golden and crisp. Spread a generous amount of the mojo picon on top of the fried bread, layer about 1 tablespoon of the seasoned pig's head mix on top and finish with the fennel fronds.

Rabbit Empanadillas

MAKES 30

When we put these empanadillas (a bite-sized version of empanadas) on our very first menu, we had to take them off again because we couldn't make them fast enough – people went nuts for them! We still pull them out every now and then as a special.

beaten free-range egg yolk, for brushing

EMPANADA DOUGH

450 g (1 lb/3 cups) cake flour, plus extra for dusting

1 teaspoon baking powder

pinch of salt

150 ml (5 fl oz) dry sherry

150 ml (5 fl oz) olive oil

RABBIT MIX

½ small farmed rabbit, jointed

salt and freshly ground black pepper

1 teaspoon ground cinnamon

1 teaspoon ground allspice, plus extra for sprinkling

splash of olive oil

2 dried bay leaves

4 garlic cloves, sliced

4 shallots, sliced

35 g (1¼ oz/¼ cup) currants

500 ml (17 fl oz/2 cups) white wine

1 litre (34 fl oz/4 cups) chicken stock

To make the empanada dough, combine the dry ingredients in a mixing bowl and form a well in the middle. Add 50 ml (1¾ fl oz) of sherry followed by 50 ml (1¾ fl oz) of oil and mix well. Repeat twice more, until all the liquid has been incorporated. Knead on the bench until soft and smooth, adding a little extra flour if needed to stop it sticking to the bench. Wrap the dough in plastic wrap and rest for at least 1 hour, either on the bench or in the fridge.

Preheat the oven to 180°C (350°F).

For the rabbit mix, season the rabbit with the salt, pepper, cinnamon and allspice. Heat a little olive oil in a large, heavy-based frying pan over a medium–high heat and brown the rabbit on all sides. Place the rabbit in a heatproof braising dish with the remaining ingredients, cover and bring to the boil over a high heat. Once boiling, transfer the dish to the oven and braise for 1 hour, or until the meat is falling off the bone. Remove the rabbit from the dish and place on a tray in the fridge to cool. Leave the oven on.

Strain the cooking liquid into a large saucepan and reserve the vegetables and currants. Bring the cooking liquid to the boil and reduce until you have a very thick glaze. Remove from the heat and put aside.

Shred the rabbit meat by hand, making sure all bones have been removed. Add the vegetable and currant mix and the glaze, and combine well.

To make the empanadas, roll 20 g (¾ oz) pieces of dough into 2-mm (⅛-in) thick rough discs, using plenty of flour for dusting. Cut each piece into a circle about 10 cm (4 in) in diameter. Place the circle over a 3 cm (1¼ in) ring and gently push the dough down into the ring, leaving some excess for folding over the filling. Fill the dough with about 1½ teaspoons of the cooled rabbit mix, push down, then enclose the filling with the dough. Turn the ring upside down and push out the empanadilla. Place on a baking tray lined with baking paper.

Once you have finished making the empanadillas, brush each one with egg yolk and sprinkle the tops with a little extra allspice. Bake in the oven for about 8 minutes, or until just brown.

PALO

E
ALL'EROS
VIAGRA
NATURALE
€ 5,00
€5,00

Vegetables & Salads

One of the joys of cooking at Bar Lourinhã is having firsthand contact with farmers. I am told so often how hard it is to be a chef, but I am very quick to point out that it's the farmer who has the hardest job of all. Farmers work ridiculously long hours and are constantly at the mercy of the gods. The changing availability of produce and the excitement approaching new seasons keeps the kitchen on its toes and ensures great diversity for plant-based tapas and raciones.

Heirloom Tomatoes, Crispy Garlic & Anchovy Sauce

SERVES 6

This is another one of our semi–Asian inspired recipes, but it's also Italian because it's based around colatura, the Italian fish sauce, that adds beautiful, salty, umami elements. It is fermented in barrels on the beach, just like in South-East Asia. If you can't get colatura, use a really good-quality Asian fish sauce.

1 kg (2 lb 3 oz) heirloom tomatoes (mixed varieties)

¼ teaspoon raw sugar

freshly ground black pepper

30 ml (1 fl oz) anchovy colatura or good-quality fish sauce

70 ml (2¼ fl oz) olive oil

15 g (½ oz/¼ cup) opal basil leaves

CRISPY GARLIC

45 g (1½ oz/½ cup) finely sliced garlic

500 ml (17 fl oz/2 cups) vegetable oil

sea salt flakes

To make the crispy garlic, combine the garlic and oil in a saucepan set over a medium heat. Slowly bring to a simmer and maintain the temperature to avoid the oil getting too hot. Cook until the garlic is brown all over, then immediately remove with a slotted spoon and place on paper towel. Once cool, salt the garlic well and store in an airtight container until needed.

To make the salad, cut the tomatoes into uneven, bite-sized shapes. Place in a mixing bowl, sprinkle with the sugar and season with pepper. Leave to sit for at least 10 minutes to macerate.

In a separate bowl or jar, combine the colatura and olive oil and mix well. Pour over enough to dress the tomatoes and store any remaining dressing in the fridge. Toss the tomatoes to coat and serve in a large sharing dish. Be sure to add all the juices that have been released from the tomatoes.

To serve, scatter over the basil leaves and crispy garlic.

Roasted Cauliflower, Walnuts & Queso de Cabra

SERVES 6

This comes from our time on Samos when we were running out of money. Cauliflower was one of the cheapest things we could buy and there were lots of them. We used to pick our own walnuts off the trees on the sides of the road, and we used a goat's milk cheese from the island. We've made it a bit more Spanish here by using queso de cabra, a firmer-style aged Spanish goat's cheese.

1 cauliflower head, cut into large florets

1 tablespoon coriander seeds, roasted and crushed

salt and freshly ground black pepper

4 tablespoons extra-virgin olive oil, plus extra for drizzling

60 g (2 oz/½ cup) roasted walnuts, crushed

¼ red onion, finely sliced

1 garlic clove, finely sliced

grated zest and juice of 2 lemons

10 g (¼ oz/⅓ cup) flat-leaf (Italian) parsley leaves, roughly torn

50 g (1¾ oz) queso de cabra (see Note)

Preheat the oven to 200°C (400°F).

Place the cauliflower florets in a large, heavy-based roasting tin and mix in the coriander seeds, some salt and pepper, the olive oil and two-thirds of the walnuts. Roast in the oven for about 25 minutes, or until slightly brown and just beginning to soften.

Remove from the oven and allow the cauliflower to cool in the roasting tin. Add the onion, garlic, lemon zest and juice and the parsley and mix together well.

To serve, put the cauliflower on a serving plate and top with shavings of the queso de cabra, the remaining walnuts and a good drizzle of olive oil. Serve either warm or at room temperature.

Note Queso de cabra is a Spanish goat's cheese that is slightly aged, but still quite creamy. You'll find it in good cheese stores and delicatessens.

Apple, Pistachio & Queso Fresco

SERVES 6

We went to a market in Tavira in Portugal and found these little house-made wheels of fresh sheep and goat's cheese, basically like a pressed ricotta. We ate the cheese with apple on a picnic one day under a tree in 40°C heat.

200 g (7 oz) queso fresco or fresh ricotta

salt and freshly ground black pepper

1 sweet apple, finely sliced and tossed in lemon juice

40 g (1½ oz/½ cup) purslane leaves (see Note)

30 g (1 oz/¼ cup) yellow inner celery leaves

2 tablespoons roasted pistachio nuts, crushed

pinch of sumac

1 tablespoon verjuice

2 tablespoons olive oil

Spoon the queso fresco into rough balls and place on a serving dish. Season well with salt and pepper. Arrange the apple slices over the cheese.

Scatter over the purslane and celery leaves, then top with the pistachios and sumac. Dress with the verjuice and olive oil.

Note Purslane is a weed-like leaf similar to a succulent that is available during the hotter months. You'll find it at good providores or farmers' markets. If you can't get hold of any, substitute it with snow pea (mangetout) shoots.

Shaved Cabbage, Labneh & Mint

SERVES 6

Labneh is a soft cheese made from strained yoghurt and it's something we always enjoyed eating and making. It comes from earlier in Matt's cooking life, a time when there was a lot of modern Middle Eastern food in Melbourne cooked by chefs like Greg Malouf. Always use a sweet young cabbage for this salad and shred it as fine as you can. It has to be super fine so the quick marinade can work and break down the cabbage so it's not just like a raw coleslaw.

1 medium sugarloaf cabbage, shredded

150 g (5½ oz) green beans, blanched and sliced on an angle

5 g (⅛ oz) golden shallots, finely sliced

¼ teaspoon caster (superfine) sugar

¼ teaspoon salt

freshly ground black pepper

5 g (⅛ oz/¼ cup) flat-leaf (Italian) parsley

5 g (⅛ oz/¼ cup) mint leaves

15 g (½ oz/¼ cup) dill

15 g (½ oz/½ cup) watercress

3 tablespoons Chardonnay vinegar, or any top-quality white-wine vinegar

8 tablespoons extra-virgin olive oil

3 tablespoons labneh, to serve

In a large mixing bowl, combine the cabbage, beans and shallots and sprinkle with the sugar, salt and some pepper to taste. Leave to sit for 15 minutes before adding the herbs, all roughly torn.

In a separate bowl, mix together the vinegar, oil and some pepper to form a dressing. Dress the salad and toss gently to coat.

Smear the labneh evenly over a large serving bowl or plate and arrange the salad on top.

Potatoes, Vinegar & Black Truffle

SERVES 6

We had this in a bar in Seville called Casablanca, a complementary course that you get when you order a meal there. We stood in this bar and ordered way too much food and then these potatoes were just put down in front of us: 'potato salad – from the house'. They were potatoes that had been cooked with stock and vinegar until they were broken down and roughly mashed. It's basically a pile of vinegary, mushy, over-flavoured potato, so we added fresh shaved truffle to take it up a notch.

- 400 g (14 oz) Nicola potatoes, peeled
- 100 ml (3½ fl oz) olive oil, plus 2 tablespoons for dressing
- 1 garlic clove, sliced
- salt and freshly ground black pepper
- approx. 1 litre (34 fl oz/4 cups) chicken stock
- 2 tablespoons sherry vinegar
- 1 small black truffle, to serve

Place the potatoes, olive oil, garlic and some salt and pepper in a saucepan and top with enough stock to just cover the potatoes. Bring to the boil, then reduce the heat and simmer for about 40 minutes, or until the potato is starting to soften. Remove from the heat.

Drain the liquid and reserve, then coarsely mash the potatoes. Add enough reserved cooking liquid to the potatoes to create a wet mash. Check and adjust the seasoning.

Slowly add the vinegar and 2 tablespoons olive oil, stirring continuously with a wooden spoon. Tip onto a serving plate and cover with finely grated black truffle.

Spiced Chickpeas & Spinach

SERVES 6

This comes from Seville. We ate it the first time in Macarena, the crazy neighbourhood to the north of the city. It's really bohemian and some of the places look a little scary to walk into but there was this smell coming out of one of them and we had never smelt that smell in Spain, let alone Europe. It was like something out of South-East Asia, punchy and heady. We went in and it was a really grubby bar with a short list and you could tell they only had a couple of things so we ordered the chickpeas with spinach. Straight after that, we walked across the road to the market, bought all of the spices, dried chickpeas and a big hearty bag of spinach leaves and took it back to our apartment and cooked it straight away. We wrote the recipe down and it has been on our menu since.

125 ml (4 fl oz/½ cup) olive oil, plus extra for frying

1 onion, roughly sliced

1 dried bay leaf

3 garlic cloves, crushed

1 tablespoon fine salt

¼ tablespoon black pepper

½ tablespoon coriander seeds, roasted and ground

½ tablespoon cumin seeds, roasted and ground

¼ tablespoon fennel seeds, roasted and ground

1 teaspoon ground allspice

1 teaspoon ground cinnamon

220 g (8 oz/1 cup) chickpeas, soaked overnight and cooked

25 g (1 oz/½ cup) silverbeet (Swiss chard), blanched and chopped (optional)

100 g (3½ oz/2 cups) English spinach

juice of 2 lemons

sea salt flakes, to serve

Heat the oil in a heavy-based saucepan over a medium heat and sweat the onion, bay leaf and garlic with the salt and pepper until the onions are translucent and soft, but not coloured. Add the spices, mix well, then remove from the heat. Mix in the chickpeas and silverbeet (if using), then transfer to the fridge to cool until ready to re-cook.

Heat a little more oil in a large frying pan over a high heat. When the oil is quite hot, add an even layer of the chickpea mixture to the pan, spreading it out to cover the base of the pan. This will allow the chickpeas to caramelise on the bottom. Do not stir or toss the mixture until the chickpeas have become quite brown, almost burnt.

Quickly add the spinach and toss or stir until it begins to soften. Remove from the heat and add the lemon juice. Serve piping hot with a sprinkle of sea salt.

smart

Mushrooms & Garlic Cream

SERVES 4

We first had this in Sydney in a funny little tapas bar we used to go to called Capitan Torres. When we were in Spain we discovered that it was a staple of most traditional tapas bars. We liked the fact that you could use a plain cultivated mushroom and turn it into something with so much flavour.

- 2 tablespoons olive oil
- 300 g (10½ oz) baby button mushrooms
- pinch of salt
- 2 garlic cloves, sliced
- 1 golden shallot, sliced
- 2 tablespoons torn flat-leaf (Italian) parsley leaves
- 125 ml (4 fl oz/½ cup) dry white wine
- 125 ml (4 fl oz/½ cup) thickened cream
- freshly ground black pepper, to taste
- 1 tablespoon toasted fine dry breadcrumbs

Heat the olive oil in a heavy, cast-iron frying pan, then add the mushrooms and salt, making sure the mushrooms are lying flat on the base of the pan. Cook on a very high heat, turning frequently, until golden brown. Add the garlic, shallot and parsley and fry until starting to soften.

Take the pan off the heat and add the wine, cream and pepper, then return the pan to a high heat and reduce and caramelise the sauce (this can take about 4–5 minutes). When the sauce has thickened and is bubbling, pour the mushrooms and sauce into a bowl and top with the toasted breadcrumbs.

Lourinhã Caipirão

½ lime

60 ml (2 fl oz/¼ cup) Liquor Beirão

ice cubes, to serve

A lighter version of a caipirinha, this has the intriguing flavours and aromas of Liquor Beirão, a Portuguese bar essential.

Muddle the lime with the Liquor Beirão in a caña. Top with ice and stir.

LIQUOR BEIRÃO

This is a Portuguese liqueur made from herbs and spices from South America, Asia and Europe.

Heirloom Carrots & PX Dressing

SERVES 6

As we connect with more and more farmers we get better and better access to really good organic produce. The carrots we use are next-level in terms of flavour. We've always loved PX sherry and the dressing here can be as sharp or as sweet as you like. It's a great play on sweet and sour with the really sweet carrots.

- 2 bunches young Dutch carrots, trimmed, peeled and washed (see Note)
- 2 tablespoons pure olive oil
- 1 teaspoon fennel seeds, roasted and ground
- salt and freshly ground black pepper
- 5 g (1/8 oz/1/4 cup) flat-leaf (Italian) parsley
- 15 g (1/2 oz/1/4 cup) dill
- 2 shallots, finely sliced
- 1 tablespoon Pedro Ximénez vinegar
- 1/2 tablespoon Pedro Ximénez sherry
- 2 tablespoons extra-virgin olive oil
- 3 tablespoons labneh, to serve

Preheat the oven to 200°C (400°F).

Place the carrots in a roasting tin and rub them with the oil, fennel seeds, salt and pepper. Roast until slightly caramelised and just cooked (test with a small knife).

Remove from the oven and allow the carrots to cool in the roasting tin before transferring to a bowl. Reserve the cooking juices for the dressing.

Roughly tear the herbs over the carrots and add the shallot.

In another bowl, whisk together the vinegar, sherry, olive oil and reserved cooking juices. Taste to check for the balance of sweetness and acidity before dressing the carrots. Gently toss to coat.

Smear the labneh over the bottom of a serving bowl or plate and heap the carrots on top.

Note Carrots can be a mixture of organic, heirloom, golf ball or Dutch carrots.

Organic Beetroot, Crème Fraîche & Liquorice

SERVES 6

This recipe was created purely because we get such good-quality beetroot now. We ate beetroot in Greece a few times. They serve them as a really simple side dish: boiled and peeled, on a plate, with vinegar poured over them. Here, we've played around a little with the crème fraîche and liquorice. Beetroot and liquorice is a really lovely combo.

- 500 g (1 lb 2 oz) good-quality organic beetroot (beets)
- 60 ml (2 fl oz/¼ cup) white vinegar
- 1 tablespoon fine salt
- 60 ml (2 fl oz/¼ cup) cava vinegar (or any good-quality white-wine vinegar)
- 50 ml (1¾ fl oz) crème fraîche
- 1 tablespoon finely chopped dill, to serve
- freshly ground black pepper, to serve
- olive oil, to serve
- liquorice, for grating

Place the beetroot in a large saucepan and cover with water. Add the white vinegar and salt and bring to the boil. Reduce the heat and simmer for about 45 minutes, or until cooked.

Drain the beetroot and allow to cool. Once cool, peel the skin using the back of a knife to create a smooth finish. Slice the beetroot into bite-sized pieces and combine with the cava vinegar in a bowl to marinate. Leave to sit for at least 30 minutes before serving.

To serve, spread the crème fraîche on a plate and place the beetroot on top. Sprinkle with dill, pepper and olive oil. Grate the liquorice over the entire dish just before serving.

{ Pictured on page 85 }

ALBARIÑO | ALVARINHO

This delicious grape from the western Spanish province of Galicia and northern tip of Portugal is a favourite of ours. It's a perfect match with vegetables. Crisp, tight and racy, albariño/alvarinhos are designed to be drunk young.

Grilled Flowering Broccoli & Almonds

SERVES 6

One of the original Bar Lourinhã dishes was a dish of green beans and almonds that we had eaten in Spain. We substituted a beautiful flowering broccoli with a nice bitterness, a purple flower and a tender juicy stem, and people loved it. Farmers' markets are the best place to source it.

- 2 bunches flowering broccoli (broccolini)
- 2 tablespoons olive oil, plus extra for marinating
- 1 tablespoon Crispy Garlic (page 68)
- 2 tablespoons flaked almonds, toasted and salted
- juice of 2 lemons
- salt and freshly ground black pepper

Blanch the broccoli in boiling salted water, then drain and refresh under cold running water for 3 minutes. Transfer to a bowl and marinate in a little olive oil and salt.

Heat a chargrill pan over a very high heat and char the broccoli evenly. Transfer to a plate and garnish with the garlic and almonds. Dress with the lemon juice, 2 tablespoons olive oil and season well with salt and pepper.

Cucumbers, Dill & Cream

SERVES 6

This recipe came about when we were visiting Berlin and went out to a traditional German restaurant for a friend's birthday. They served chunks of peeled cucumbers marinated in vinegar and dill in a bowl of thickened cream and it was really, really good. We added some verjuice to the cream in our version to lightly acidulate it.

- 125 ml (4 fl oz/½ cup) thickened cream
- salt and freshly ground black pepper
- 2 teaspoons verjuice
- 4 kipfler (fingerling) potatoes, boiled, peeled and sliced
- 2 Lebanese (short) cucumbers, peeled
- 1 golden shallot, sliced
- 1 tablespoon lemon juice
- 30 g (1 oz/½ cup) dill, torn
- extra-virgin olive oil, for drizzling

Mix together the cream, ¼ teaspoon pepper, some salt and the verjuice in a bowl. Refrigerate until ready to serve.

To serve, pour the cream into the base of a serving bowl and arrange the potatoes on top.

Using a wide peeler, shave the cucumbers into another bowl. Add the shallot, lemon juice and some salt. Mix well, then heap on top of the potatoes.

Finish the salad with the dill, plenty of freshly ground pepper and a drizzle of olive oil.

Smoked Eggplant, Hazelnut & Green Chilli

SERVES 6

This is straight out of Samos. We used to get eggplants and rub them in olive oil and salt and pop them on the embers of a fire to cook. Normally, the pulp would go straight into a baba ganoush, but at Bar Lourinhã, we cook it so it still holds its shape and you get beautiful chunks of smoked eggplant.

3 medium-sized eggplants (aubergines)

olive oil

salt and freshly ground black pepper

½ green chilli, finely sliced

5 g (⅛ oz/¼ cup) flat-leaf (Italian) parsley leaves

15 g (½ oz/½ cup) coriander (cilantro) leaves

1 tablespoon roasted hazelnuts, crushed

¼ teaspoon pink peppercorns, crushed

DRESSING

1 tablespoon red-wine vinegar

¼ teaspoon raw (demerara) sugar

3 tablespoons olive oil

1 garlic clove, finely sliced

For the dressing, mix the vinegar, sugar, olive oil and sliced garlic in a bowl. Leave to sit until needed.

Use a skewer to pierce the eggplants, making sure they are evenly pricked all over. Rub a little olive oil on the eggplants and season well with salt. Place on a barbecue chargrill plate, in a chargrill pan or over a naked gas flame and cook, turning continuously, until the skin is blackened and the eggplant is cooked. Place in a bowl to cool and add any liquid that draws out of the eggplant to the dressing.

Halve the eggplants lengthways and gently peel. Arrange in a serving dish and season well.

Loosely scatter the chilli, parsley, coriander and hazelnut over the eggplant. Dress generously, then finish with the pink peppercorns.

Baby Lettuce, Anchovy & Aioli

SERVES 6

We first came across cogollos in Valencia on our first trip to Spain. We had no idea what it was but instead of asking, we just ordered it. It came out as a beautiful salad topped with really good Cantabrian anchovies, piquillo peppers and flaked bonito tuna dressed with oil and juices from the tin. The 'cogollos' refers to the perfect little lettuce hearts, cut in half. Whenever we can get cogollos from the farmers, we put it on the menu. Use the best anchovies you can get – don't sacrifice.

1 tablespoon Aioli (page 166)

3 baby iceberg or cos (romaine) lettuce hearts, quartered lengthways

8 anchovy fillets, halved lengthways

8 cornichons, sliced

10 caperberries, slivered

1 golden shallot, sliced

1 teaspoon lemon thyme leaves

salt and freshly ground black pepper

DRESSING

1 tablespoon Chardonnay vinegar, or good-quality white-wine vinegar

3 tablespoons extra-virgin olive oil

salt and freshly ground black pepper

Spread the aioli onto a serving plate and arrange the lettuce hearts on top. Sprinkle with the anchovies, cornichons, caperberries, shallot, thyme and seasoning. To finish, mix the dressing ingredients well and pour over the salad.

{ Pictured on page 123 }

Seafood

Selecting the finest seafood is a delicate balance between affordability, sustainability and great communication with your fishmonger. We have had an ongoing relationship with John and George from Ocean Made Seafood in Melbourne; they understand our needs and also share our commitment to quality. Not all seafood in this chapter is available all year round, so have a chat with your fish supplier before deciding what recipe you want to cook. We normally only list two seafood dishes on our menu, but we have a conversation with John and George each morning and order what has just come in to supplement the menu with additional seafood dishes.

Tuna 'Lomo' & Almonds

SERVES 6

We first served this a few years ago when you could get tuna at a reasonable price – that's really hard to do now, which is a good thing because the price reflects the fact that it's being fished sustainably. The almond sauce is loosely based on an almond sauce we had in Cádiz, but that one was always served with meat. We thought it would be a great fit with the richness of the tuna. You can use other types of fish like albacore. The flavour is still good, though you don't get the brilliant colour of the yellowfin.

40 g (1½ oz/¼ cup) raw whole almonds, to serve

olive oil

snow pea (mangetout) shoots or wild leaves such as amaranth, rocket (arugula) or chickweed

salt and freshly ground black pepper

TUNA 'LOMO'

1 tablespoon sweet paprika

1 tablespoon sea salt flakes

1 teaspoon freshly cracked black pepper

1 teaspoon caster (superfine) sugar

1 teaspoon ground allspice

300 g (10½ oz) yellowfin tuna loin

ALMOND SAUCE

45 g (1½ oz/½ cup) flaked almonds, toasted

250 ml (8½ fl oz/1 cup) thickened cream

1 shallot, sliced

1 garlic clove, sliced

3 tablespoons olive oil

salt and freshly ground black pepper

For the tuna lomo, combine the dry ingredients in a bowl and rub the mixture into the tuna loin. Wrap the tuna in plastic wrap and refrigerate for about 30 minutes.

After 30 minutes, remove the fish from the plastic wrap and lightly pat dry with paper towel, being careful not to remove too much of the cure. Re-wrap in plastic wrap and refrigerate until ready to serve.

To make the almond sauce, combine all the ingredients in a saucepan and quickly bring to the boil. Remove from the heat and allow to cool before blending to a smooth sauce. Refrigerate until ready to serve.

Preheat the oven to 180°C (350°F).

Combine the almonds with a little oil and salt in a roasting tin and roast in the oven until toasted. Allow to cool, then crush in a mortar and pestle.

Arrange some almond sauce on a serving plate and lay fine slices of tuna on top. Garnish with the snow pea shoots, crushed nuts, a little extra salt and pepper and a drizzle of olive oil.

Kingfish 'Pancetta'

SERVES 6

This has been on offer at Bar Lourinhã from day one. Although we have recently removed it from the menu, our regulars know that it's always available as an off-menu addition. The initial version came about while we were in Noosa, but it really came into its own once we'd been to Spain, particularly after tasting mojama for the first time in Murcia. It was the texture more than the flavour that grabbed us, and that's what we wanted to come to the fore with this one. The lemon oil is what pulls it all together. It's an oil that's made in Tuscany and it has a viscosity that's incredible.

'PANCETTA' SPICE MIX

65 g (2¼ oz/½ cup) sea salt

¾ teaspoon sweet paprika

¼ teaspoon ground allspice

¼ teaspoon ground cloves

¼ teaspoon ground cinnamon

1 teaspoon freshly ground black pepper, plus extra to serve

1 teaspoon caster (superfine) sugar

3 teaspoons finely chopped lemon thyme

400 g (14 oz) yellowtail kingfish (preferably belly), skin, bones and bloodline removed

TO SERVE

2 teaspoons chopped lemon thyme

1 small red onion, finely sliced

extra-virgin lemon oil

Gently combine the salt, spices, sugar and lemon thyme in a bowl. Roll and pat the kingfish in the spices, then wrap in plastic wrap and refrigerate for 3 hours.

Remove the kingfish from the plastic wrap, pat dry with paper towel, then wrap the fish in a piece of muslin (cheesecloth) and store for up to 5 days in the fridge.

When you're ready to serve, use a sharp carving knife to cut the kingfish into thin slices. Arrange on a serving plate and scatter over the lemon thyme, red onion and a sprinkling of pepper. Finish with a generous splash of lemon oil.

Blue Mackerel 'Escabeche'

SERVES 6

The first time we had escabeche was in Granada. Granada is the home of free tapas, and so, when you walk into a bar and buy a beer, they give you a plate of something. It might just be olives or nuts, but in this bar in the Albaicín district, it was a couple of sardines that had been fried and then popped into an earthenware jar with some vinegar and saffron. It just sat on the bench, not refrigerated or anything. They scooped the fish out with a bit of pickled vegetable. This was something we made at Bar Lourinhã from the beginning. You can use the escabeche to dress fish straight away, or sear the fish and leave it in the escabeche to serve the following day or the day after.

olive oil, for frying

fennel fronds, to garnish

MACKEREL

6 blue mackerel fillets

grated zest of 1 lemon

pinch of lemon thyme leaves

pinch of oregano leaves

salt and freshly ground black pepper

ESCABECHE

125 ml (4 fl oz/½ cup) extra-virgin olive oil

10 shallots, finely sliced

2 garlic cloves, finely sliced

1 tablespoon coriander seeds, crushed

1 teaspoon ground allspice

1 teaspoon ground cinnamon

2 teaspoons saffron threads, lightly toasted and crushed

60 ml (2 fl oz/¼ cup) Chardonnay vinegar or good-quality white-wine vinegar

salt and freshly ground black pepper

To prepare the mackerel, rub the fish with the lemon zest, lemon thyme, oregano, salt and pepper. Cover with plastic wrap and chill in the fridge for up to 10 hours.

For the escabeche, heat the oil in a heavy-based frying pan over a low heat and fry the shallots and garlic until just softened but not coloured. Remove from the heat and mix in the remaining ingredients. The escabeche can be made up to 1 week in advance if kept in the fridge.

To serve, pat the fish dry with paper towel. Heat a little oil in a large frying pan over a high heat and sear the fillets for no more than 1½ minutes on each side. Place in a deep serving dish and pour the escabeche over the fish.

Serve either hot or at room temperature and garnish with plenty of fennel fronds.

Shark & Waxy Spuds

SERVES 6

We came across this dish in a seaside town in the south of Spain called Sanlúcar de Barrameda. We'd been to La Goya, the sherry house, and they told us we had to go to this bar in the square. They served us this dish made with dogfish – a large, very gelatinous fish – that seemed like southern Spanish fish and chips in its most rustic form. The potatoes had been cooked whole with the oil of the fish. So it was confit-like fish, potatoes that had been randomly smashed and onions. It was bitey and ballsy and loaded with texture and had a crunchy bottom. It went straight onto our menu.

300 g (10½ oz) King Edward potatoes, peeled and cut into large chunks

peel of 1 lemon

1 dried bay leaf

2 tablespoons thyme, roughly torn

2 tablespoons oregano, roughly torn

2 garlic cloves, finely sliced

salt and freshly ground black pepper

blended olive oil (enough to cover the potatoes)

200 g (7 oz) firm white fish fillet, such as gummy shark

½ red onion, finely sliced

3 spring onions (scallions), finely sliced

50 ml (1¾ fl oz) lemon juice

Preheat the oven to 160°C (320°F).

Place the potatoes, lemon peel, bay leaf, thyme, oregano, garlic and some salt and pepper in a deep, ovenproof frying pan and cover with the oil. Place the pan over a medium–low heat and heat slowly until just bubbling. Cover with a lid and transfer to the oven. Cook for about 45 minutes, or until the potatoes are just cooked.

Remove from the oven and place in a warm spot. Place the shark on top of the potatoes and allow to slowly cook through over a very low heat for about 45 minutes to 1 hour. Remove the shark and potatoes from the oil and gently smash the potatoes and flake the fish.

Mix the shark and potatoes gently with a little of the flavoured cooking oil, the red onion, spring onions and lemon juice. Arrange on a serving plate and serve warm.

Roasted Sardines, Bread & Parsley

SERVES 6

You can get fresh sardines from the market or your local fish shop and we recommend you do because if we don't support our local fishmongers, we're all going to end up having to buy frozen stuff from the supermarket. That's the reality everywhere.

18 sardine fillets

olive oil, for greasing and drizzling

salt and freshly ground black pepper

25 g (1 oz/⅓ cup) toasted finely torn fresh breadcrumbs, to serve

PARSLEY & BREAD SAUCE

2 slices stale sourdough bread, crusts removed

40 g (1½ oz/2 cups) flat-leaf (Italian) parsley leaves

1 shallot, chopped

1 garlic clove, crushed

100 ml (3½ fl oz) lemon juice

100 ml (3½ fl oz) olive oil

salt and freshly ground black pepper

To make the sauce, combine all the ingredients in a blender and blend to a smooth green paste. Add a little water if necessary to loosen the mixture. Set aside.

Preheat the oven to 220°C (430°F).

To cook the sardines, arrange them on a well-oiled baking tray and season with salt and pepper. Roast in the oven for 3–4 minutes.

Transfer the sardines to a serving plate and top with a spoonful of the parsley and bread sauce. Finish with a drizzle of olive oil and the toasted breadcrumbs.

Arroz a Banda

SERVES 6

This is a traditional dish from Catalonia – it's fishermen's fare. They'd fillet their fish and be left with all the bones, so they'd make a soup with them, chuck in a couple of tomatoes, a head of garlic and then cook rice and eat that on the boat. We had a lot of different versions of this. I just wanted to do something simple here, but we made it a bit fancier with the prawns roasted into the top of it.

12 medium, whole raw prawns (shrimp)

6 lemon wedges, to serve

sea salt, to serve

pimentón, for dusting

RICE

100 ml (3½ fl oz) olive oil, plus extra for drizzling

2 tablespoons crushed garlic

1 onion, roughly diced

3 Bull's Horn peppers, diced

1 tablespoon pimentón

350 g (12½ oz) bomba rice (see Note)

2 litres (68 fl oz/8 cups) fish stock

For the rice, heat the oil in a saucepan and gently sweat the garlic, onion and peppers until very soft. Add the pimentón, mix well, then add the rice.

Increase the heat to high and add 1.5 litres (51 fl oz/6 cups) of the fish stock. Bring to the boil, then lower the heat to medium and cook, stirring constantly, until the rice just begins to soften. Remove from the heat and allow to cool. Once cool, add the remaining stock and allow to absorb. The rice mixture should be quite moist at this stage.

Preheat the oven to 200°C (400°F).

Transfer the rice to a 30–40 cm (12–16 in) paella pan or large, shallow ovenproof frying pan, and arrange the prawns in a decorative pattern on top. Push the prawns lightly into the rice.

Set the pan on a large burner over a high heat and cook until the rice begins to bubble. Transfer to the oven and cook for 7–9 minutes, or until the prawns are just cooked.

Serve immediately with lemon wedges, a sprinkle of sea salt, a drizzle of olive oil and a dusting of pimentón.

Note Bomba rice is an extremely short-grain rice, almost round, with incredible absorption abilities. It's also extremely forgiving when cooking.

Stuffed Calamari

SERVES 8

We played around with this recipe in Samos because we had plenty of access to fresh calamari and there was usually leftover bread lying around. This has jamón through it though, on the island, we were doing it with bread and currants and lots of olive oil. You can put anything in it. Nuts are great, fruit is great, but the jamón is really interesting because it doesn't take the full brunt of the heat so doesn't overcook and it adds a beautiful jamón perfume to the dish.

4 medium-sized whole calamari (no longer than 20 cm/8 in)

lemon wedges, to serve

STUFFING

200 g (7 oz) torn stale sourdough bread

1 garlic clove, sliced

40 g (1½ oz/¼ cup) chopped jamón serrano

2 tablespoons chopped flat-leaf (Italian) parsley

grated zest and juice of 1 lemon

2 tablespoons extra-virgin olive oil, plus extra for drizzling

salt and freshly ground black pepper

Clean the calamari by removing the wings and tentacles. Turn the tube inside out and remove any innards, then set aside.

For the stuffing, chop the calamari wings and tentacles and combine in a bowl with the remaining ingredients. Carefully fill each calamari tube and close with a toothpick.

Heat a barbecue chargrill plate or chargrill pan over a high heat. Grill the calamari for about 3 minutes each side, then slice and serve with lemon wedges and a drizzle of olive oil.

Mussel Cataplana

SERVES 6

Cataplana is a traditional Portuguese cooking vessel. It's made out of copper and has a hinged lid. You start off with a basic sofrito in the bottom of the pot, chuck in your seafood and a splash of wine then close it tight and throw it on the heat. It stays closed until it's brought to the table where it gets popped open and a beautiful aroma wafts out. If you don't have access to a cataplana, you can use a pot with a decent lid that seals properly and looks presentable so you can lift the lid at the table and get the same effect.

1 kg (2 lb 3 oz) fresh mussels, washed and de-bearded

125 ml (4 fl oz/½ cup) white wine

SOFRITO

60 ml (2 fl oz/¼ cup) extra-virgin olive oil

1 Bull's Horn pepper or capsicum (bell pepper), finely diced

3 shallots, finely chopped

1 dried bay leaf

salt and freshly ground black pepper

125 g (4½ oz/½ cup) chopped dried chorizo

1 teaspoon pimentón

5 g (⅛ oz) chopped flat-leaf (Italian) parsley

For the sofrito, heat the oil in a cataplana or large saucepan and fry the pepper, shallot and bay leaf. Season and continue cooking until the pepper has softened. Remove from the heat and add the chorizo, pimentón and parsley.

Add the mussels to the sofrito and stir well, then pour in the white wine and immediately seal the cataplana or saucepan with a lid. Cook for 3–4 minutes.

Serve in the cataplana at the table or in a serving bowl if using a saucepan. Discard any mussels that remain closed.

LIMONES
UROS KILO

ajos
100 1/4
ajos
ajos
ajos
ajos
120 1/4

Mussels, Burnt Butter & Bread Sauce

SERVES 6

We're not sure where Matt came up with this idea of burnt butter and bread but, over the past few years, he's been using more bread in sauces than ever. Before that, he used a lot of nuts to thicken sauces and, before that, it was flour. Use the freshest, plumpest mussels you can find for this recipe and cook them very quickly so they stay juicy. Also try and get the freshest, best-quality pimentón you can lay your hands on. It should have an almost floral aroma of smoke and pepper.

- 50 ml (1¾ fl oz) olive oil, plus extra to garnish
- 1 garlic clove, crushed
- 1 kg (2 lb 3 oz) mussels, washed and de-bearded
- 100 ml (3½ fl oz) dry white wine
- 1 teaspoon pimentón, to garnish

BURNT BUTTER & BREAD SAUCE

- 250 g (9 oz/1 cup) butter
- 1 garlic clove, sliced
- 1 shallot, sliced
- small pinch of ground cinnamon
- 200 g (7 oz) bread, torn and soaked in water
- salt and freshly ground black pepper

To make the sauce, heat the butter in frying pan until it becomes a nut-brown colour (beurre noisette), then add the garlic, shallot and cinnamon before it reaches burning point. Transfer to a cold bowl or heatproof container to stop the cooking process, then leave to cool.

Combine the soaked bread with a little of its soaking water in a blender and blitz to form a paste. While blending, slowly add the burnt butter and season well. Refrigerate until ready to serve.

Heat the oil in a large, heavy-based stockpot and add the garlic and mussels. When the mussels are very hot and sizzling, add the wine and cover with a lid. Cook for 3–4 minutes, or until the mussels have opened. Discard any mussels that remain closed.

Remove from the heat and place the mussels in serving bowl, removing one of each mussel's shells so the mussel sits in a half-shell.

Add 3 tablespoons burnt butter sauce to the pot and whisk until a smooth sauce forms. Any leftover butter can be stored in an airtight container in the refrigerator and used for thickening sauces. Pour a generous amount of sauce over the mussels and garnish with a fine sifting of pimentón and a splash of olive oil.

Prawn & Saffron Açorda

SERVES 4

We got this recipe from Iberian wine importer Scott Wasley who got it from a Portuguese winemaker. It's like a bread porridge with seafood in it. It's a classic peasant dish, designed to be as robust and filling as possible. It's normally served with a fresh egg yolk right at the end, but we decided a big dollop of aioli over the top would work pretty well. Every time we serve this, the plates come back completely empty, licked clean.

3 tablespoons olive oil, plus extra to serve

3 garlic cloves, sliced

2 shallots, sliced

8 medium-sized raw prawns (shrimp), peeled and chopped

100 g (3½ oz/1 cup) torn sourdough bread, crusts removed

¼ teaspoon toasted saffron threads

500 ml (17 fl oz/2 cups) fish stock

grated zest and juice of 1 lemon

2 tablespoons Aioli (page 164), to serve

¼ teaspoon chilli flakes, to garnish

15 g (½ oz/½ cup) coriander (cilantro) leaves, to garnish

Heat the olive oil in a large saucepan and gently sweat the garlic and shallot until soft, then add the prawns. Cook over a medium heat until the prawns turn orange.

Add the bread and saffron, stir to combine, then add three-quarters of the fish stock and the lemon zest and juice. Increase the heat to high and bring to the boil. Cook for a further 2–3 minutes until it starts to resemble a porridge-like consistency. Add more stock if it's too dry.

To serve, divide between individual bowls with a dollop of aioli, a sprinkle of chilli flakes, some coriander leaves and a good glug of olive oil.

Clams, Fino & Ancho Chilli

SERVES 6

Murcia is a non-tourist town in Andalusia about half an hour inland from the coast. We knew nothing about it but it turned out that the food culture there was really, really strong. Gran Bar didn't even look like a bar – it was just an open door really – but we heard some noise and saw a couple of old blokes walk out laughing so we decided to go in. It was a bar from the 1940s, run by a man and his nephew with food arranged on the bar. There was a bowl of live clams that were all open and every time the old man walked past them he would clap at them and they'd close. This dish reminds me of that bar. We use fino here instead of wine because it is drier and it works well with the ancho.

- 2 tablespoons olive oil, plus extra to serve
- 3 shallots, finely sliced
- 2 garlic cloves, finely sliced
- 1 kg (2 lb 3 oz) small fresh clams
- 125 ml (4 fl oz/½ cup) fino sherry
- 1 teaspoon ground ancho chilli, to serve (see Notes)

Heat the oil in a large stockpot over a medium heat and sweat the shallot and garlic until soft but not coloured. Increase the heat to high and add the clams, moving a little bit to evenly distribute the shallot and garlic.

When the clams are hot and sizzling, add the sherry and immediately cover with a lid, being careful to avoid any flames from the sherry. Cook for 3–5 minutes, or until at least three-quarters of the clams have opened, then remove from the heat. Using tongs, pry open the remaining closed clams (see Notes).

Using a slotted spoon, transfer the clams to a serving bowl and arrange the shells so their 'mouths' are facing up. Pour over the cooking liquid and dust with a little ancho chilli and a squirt of olive oil.

Notes Clams that have not opened are fine to eat. In today's quality-controlled world, there is only a very small chance of them being bad. The main reason for clams not opening is due to very strong adductor muscles and not enough heat. You may need to give them some help to open using an oyster knife or a teaspoon.

Ancho chilli is a dried poblano chilli that has an interesting bitter, smoky and gentle warm flavour.

Soft-shell Prawns al Ajillo

SERVES 4

These garlic prawns just walk out the door. We serve them in sizzling hot pans. You walk through the restaurant with the pans and if people haven't ordered them already, they all say, 'I want that'. The dish is at such a temperature that the prawns are still crackling when you put it on the table and people just look at it and go, 'How do I get my mouth on that', because it's so hot. Handle with care. Must be served with crispy bread and ice-cold fino.

- 8 medium-sized whole prawns (shrimp)
- 25 ml (¾ fl oz) blended olive oil
- pinch of sea salt flakes
- 75 ml (2½ fl oz) extra-virgin olive oil
- 1 teaspoon chilli flakes
- 1 tablespoon finely chopped flat-leaf (Italian) parsley
- 2 garlic cloves, crushed
- juice of 2 lemons
- crispy bread and ice-cold fino sherry, to serve

Preheat the oven to 200°C (400°F).

Place the prawns in a large, ovenproof frying pan so they are lying perfectly flat, then add the blended oil and salt. Set the pan over a high heat and cook until the prawns start to turn orange. Turn the prawns over and transfer the pan to the oven. Cook for about 5 minutes, or until the prawns are cooked through.

Place the pan back on the stove over a medium heat. Add the extra-virgin olive oil, chilli, parsley and garlic and cook until the garlic just starts to change colour.

Remove from the heat, add the lemon juice and serve immediately with crispy bread and a glass of fino.

Garfish Caldeirada

SERVES 4

This dish is a little more refined than what you would eat in Portugal where it's very rustic, messy and full of bones. We use boned whole fish (but you can use boned fillets too) and serve it in a bowl alongside all the things it was cooked with. If you can't get garfish you can use mackerel or sardines.

- 60 ml (2 fl oz/¼ cup) olive oil, plus extra to serve
- 5 shallots, roughly diced
- 2 garlic cloves, chopped
- 2 teaspoons ground cumin
- 75 g (2¾ oz/1 cup) chopped fennel
- salt and freshly ground black pepper
- 4 ripe tomatoes, peeled, seeded and chopped
- 500 ml (17 fl oz/2 cups) fish stock
- 4 Nicola potatoes, boiled, peeled and halved
- 4 whole garfish
- coriander (cilantro) leaves, to garnish

Heat the oil in a wide, heavy-based saucepan and sweat the shallot, garlic, cumin, fennel and some salt and pepper until soft. Add the tomatoes and cook until the mixture is slightly dry.

Add the stock and potatoes and bring to a simmer. Add the garfish and cook for about 6 minutes, ensuring the fillets are slightly submerged in the soup.

Remove the fish and potatoes and place in a serving bowl. Pour over enough soup to cover the fish, then garnish with coriander and finish with a dash of olive oil.

Chilli-roasted Blue Crab

SERVES 6

When we were in Noosa we used to have a crab night and fell in love with blue crabs. They have a sweet flavour and are so, so good. They can be a bit tricky to get into, but it's worth it for the sweetness. And, anyway, we like to get a bit dirty with crabs, like they do in Spain. You will need bibs and all the paraphernalia for this one. Our customers turn into slobbering messes when eating these and we love that – it's beautiful to see people enjoying food so much. This dish also goes incredibly well with cava.

4 blue crabs, quartered, cap and dead man's fingers removed

60 ml (2 fl oz/¼ cup) extra-virgin olive oil, plus extra for roasting

pinch of salt

4 garlic cloves, finely sliced

2 shallots, finely sliced

6 long dried chillies, broken in half

20 g (¾ oz/1 cup) flat-leaf (Italian) parsley leaves, roughly torn

juice of 2 lemons

Preheat the oven to 200°C (400°F).

Place the crabs in a heavy-based roasting tin with some olive oil and the salt. Heat the tin on the stove, then transfer to the oven. Roast the crabs for 5 minutes, then turn and continue roasting for another 5 minutes.

Remove the tin from the oven and put back on the stovetop over a low heat. Add the olive oil, garlic, shallot, chilli and parsley and cook until the garlic softens. Add the lemon juice and serve immediately.

Twice-cooked Octopus

SERVES 6

We first tried this in Sakkouleika, the hillside village on Samos where Jo's family comes from. The family was making ouzo and souma in the family still that's heated with coal and wood. There was a grill outside – basically an iron box – that they shovelled coals from the still into. The village priest appeared out of nowhere with two foil-wrapped parcels containing whole octopus, lemon, garlic, wild herbs and salt that he threw on the grill. It's known in the village that the priest always brings the best octopus, so everybody was happy he'd showed up. The foil quickly puffed up like a balloon with the steam and then the priest removed the foil and threw the octopus directly onto the grill. The octopus is already tenderised with the lemon and salt, but with the steaming and grilling it gets ridiculously soft and juicy. We drank a lot of souma, so it's surprising we remembered the recipe.

2 kg (4 lb 6 oz) octopus (the larger the better)

olive oil, for rubbing and drizzling

sea salt flakes and lemon cheeks, to serve

MARINADE

4 garlic cloves

1 tablespoon salt

2 teaspoons freshly cracked black pepper

2 lemons, juiced and sliced

1 small onion, roughly sliced

½ bunch thyme stalks

250 ml (8½ fl oz/1 cup) dry white wine

Start the octopus a day ahead. Remove the head (if still attached) and the tentacles from one another. Place the octopus in a plastic container with all the marinade ingredients, cover and refrigerate overnight.

In the morning, or 1 hour before serving, create a foil parcel by layering three large sheets of foil on a bench with a small amount of oil between each layer to stick them together. Place the octopus and its marinade on the bottom half of the foil and fold over the top half, being careful not to lose any of the juices. Tightly press and twist the edges together to secure (similar to closing pastry on a pie).

Make sure the parcel is watertight, then place it on a scorching hot barbecue chargrill plate for 1 hour. When it balloons up (after roughly 5 minutes), lower the heat and continue cooking until the hour is up.

Remove the octopus from the foil, discarding the marinade. Turn the grill back to high, lightly rub the octopus tentacles with oil and grill for 2–3 minutes on each side, or until nicely charred.

Serve on a platter with sprigs of oregano, a pinch of sea salt and lemon cheeks. Drizzle with a splash of olive oil.

UZO

LANGOSTINOS
GORDO
3 1/4

Pipis & Coriander Butter

SERVES 6

Matt's never been a fan of pipis. They can be tough and sometimes sandy and not quite fresh enough. But you can get really good pipis now. We ate a plate of these on the beach in Portugal. They'd been cooked over fire in a mixture of oil and butter, which is unusual because they rarely cook with butter in Spain. There were also handfuls of torn coriander and some lemon. So simple but so good. If you can't get pipis, clams will work just as well.

2 tablespoons olive oil

2 shallots, finely sliced

1 garlic clove, finely sliced

1 teaspoon crushed coriander seeds

1 kg (2 lb 3 oz) smooth-shell pipis or clams

100 ml (3½ fl oz) dry white wine

7 g (⅛ oz/¼ cup) coriander (cilantro) leaves, torn

CORIANDER BUTTER

100 g (3½ oz) unsalted butter

½ bunch coriander (cilantro) leaves and stalks

25 ml (¾ fl oz) thickened cream

freshly ground black pepper, to taste

To make the coriander butter, soften the butter at room temperature, being careful not to let it melt. Blanch the coriander in salted boiling water for 15 seconds, then refresh in a bowl of iced water. Squeeze out all the excess water and roughly chop.

Combine the butter and coriander in a food processor and blend until smooth, then add the cream and pepper to taste. Mix well and refrigerate until needed.

Combine the olive oil, shallot, garlic and coriander seed in a heavy-based saucepan over a low heat. Cook until the shallot is soft but not coloured. Increase the heat to high and add the pipis. Stir well and, when the pipis are very hot, add the wine. Immediately cover with a lid and cook for around 5 minutes, or until the pipis have opened.

Remove from the heat and add 3 tablespoons of coriander butter and the torn coriander. Serve immediately, pouring plenty of sauce over the pipis.

Meat

Availability of ethically raised animals and environmentally responsible farming is more widespread now than when we opened, and we encourage you to seek out good options at your butcher or farmers' market. Using the whole animal has always been a priority for us, and we have served offal since our very first menu. We invest a lot of time researching and learning about where our meat comes from and we enjoy passing this information on to our customers.

Wagyu 'Carne Cruda' & Shaved Beetroot

SERVES 6

In 2005, we were heading north in Italy to visit family and we stopped in Piedmont with Matt's parents. We were staying in a five-house town with one osteria across the road. We ate at the osteria three nights and Matt ate the carne crudo three nights in a row. We'd had steak tartare before, but we were just intrigued how this simple seasoned ball of flavoursome meat and olive oil could be so good. They served it with a plate of root vegetables. We serve ours with fresh horseradish, beetroot and a little bit of bread.

50 g (1¾ oz) piece of fresh horseradish, peeled, to garnish

CARNE CRUDA

300 g (10½ oz) wagyu topside

grated zest of 1 lemon

1 shallot, very finely diced

3 tablespoons lemon oil

salt and freshly ground black pepper

SALAD

3 baby beetroot (beets), finely shaved

3 small red radishes, finely shaved

5 g (⅛ oz/¼ cup) young flat-leaf (Italian) parsley leaves

2 teaspoons oregano leaves

¼ red onion, finely sliced

2 tablespoons lemon oil, plus extra for drizzling

salt and freshly ground black pepper, to taste

For the carne cruda, finely dice or mince the beef no more than 30 minutes before serving. Add the lemon zest, shallot, lemon oil and some salt and pepper and mix well. Check the seasoning and set aside.

To make the salad, gently toss all the salad ingredients together in a bowl and season to taste with salt and pepper.

To serve, briskly work the meat with a large serving spoon, form it into a smooth ball and place it on a serving plate. Arrange the salad alongside the meat and dress it with a little more lemon oil. Shave a generous amount of horseradish over the entire dish just before serving.

V

Chicken Livers, Sherry & Almonds

SERVES 6

We had this in a couple of places, mostly in Jerez in the south of Spain, especially with the almonds. It's one of the more traditional recipes at Bar Lourinhã where we haven't really tried to do anything different. It's just about classic flavours.

1 tablespoon olive oil

300 g (10½ oz) free-range, hand-picked chicken livers, cleaned

salt and freshly ground black pepper

1 dried bay leaf

1 garlic clove, finely sliced

2 shallots, finely sliced

1 tablespoon sherry vinegar

60 ml (2 fl oz/¼ cup) dry sherry

125 ml (4 fl oz/½ cup) chicken stock

2 tablespoons cold butter

10 g (¼ oz/½ cup) flat-leaf (Italian) parsley leaves, torn

30 g (1 oz/⅓ cup) flaked almonds, toasted, to garnish

Heat the oil in a large, heavy-based saucepan, then place the chicken livers face down in the pan. Cook over a high heat until brown, turning with tongs.

Season the livers well before adding the bay leaf, garlic and shallot. Cook until the liver is well browned.

Add the vinegar, sherry and chicken stock and cook until slightly thickened. Reduce the heat to low and add the butter and parsley, stirring until the butter has been incorporated into the sauce.

When the livers begin to feel slightly firm – around 4–5 minutes – remove them from the pan and arrange on a serving dish. Cover with the sauce and garnish with the flaked almonds.

S. EGIDIO PREGATE PER
SAINT EGIDIO PRAY

Morcilla Tortillas

SERVES 6

We went to a breakfast bar called Felino close to the Valencia market, a really nice place run by a brother and sister. Every day they would have a different type of tortilla. Until then, we'd only seen traditional tortilla Espanola. It was quite refreshing to see them put different sorts of things in their tortilla, and we'd go there every day. There was a beautiful leek and anchovy, a morcilla one, a chorizo one, a bacalhau one. We were inspired that you could put anything with eggs and potatoes and call it a tortilla.

5 free-range eggs

5 tablespoons thickened cream

salt and freshly ground black pepper

olive oil, for frying

1 Nicola potato, boiled, peeled and diced

1 garlic clove, finely sliced

1 morcilla sausage, cut into 5 mm (¼ in) slices

3 large tablespoons Aioli, to serve (page 164)

1 teaspoon pimentón, to garnish

Preheat the oven to 200°C (400°F). Beat the eggs, cream and some salt and pepper in a bowl, then set aside.

Heat two 12 cm (4¾ in) non-stick ovenproof blini pans with about 2 mm (1/16 in) of olive oil. Add the potato and garlic and fry until heated through. Remove from the heat and add enough egg mixture to fill three-quarters of each pan.

Return to the heat and gently move the egg from the bottom and side of the pan until the egg is lightly cooked but still a little runny. Press the slices of morcilla into the top of the tortillas in a ring around the edge. Transfer to the oven and cook until the egg is just set.

Serve hot, with a dollop of aioli on the side and a sprinkling of pimentón on top.

Salted Pork & Giant Clams

SERVES 6

This is an all-time favourite, one of the great surf and turf combinations. We had this dish in Tavira and it blew us away. The sauce is sticky and delicious. We salt the pork overnight and cook it very slowly.

- 1 tablespoon sea salt
- 1/4 tablespoon ground allspice
- 1/4 tablespoon whole black peppercorns
- 1 teaspoon brown sugar
- 2 garlic cloves, crushed
- 150 g (5 1/2 oz) pork belly, diced
- 100 ml (3 1/2 fl oz) olive oil, plus extra to serve
- 5 shallots, peeled and halved (or quartered if large)
- 1/4 cinnamon stick
- 1 dried bay leaf
- 2 teaspoons sweet paprika
- 1 kg (2 lb 3 oz) large clams, soaked (see Note)
- 150 ml (5 fl oz) white wine
- 2 tablespoons chopped flat-leaf (Italian) parsley
- salt and freshly ground black pepper
- juice of 1 lemon, to serve

Combine the sea salt, allspice, peppercorns, sugar and garlic in a bowl, then rub the marinade into the diced pork belly and set aside for at least 1 hour.

In a large, heavy-based stockpot, heat the oil over medium heat and fry the pork with the shallots until the shallots have softened. Add the cinnamon, bay leaf and sweet paprika and season well.

Add the clams to the pot, increase the heat to high, then add the white wine and chopped parsley. Immediately seal with a lid and cook until the clams are just open. Serve in a large dish with the lemon juice and a generous amount of olive oil over the top.

Note Tasmania produces some of the best large clams I have tasted. Strawberry clams from Eden in New South Wales are also a favourite of mine.

Roasted House Morcilla, Red Pepper & Free-range Egg

SERVES 8

We had a revelation in the town of Murcia. We went to this bar and had the most rustic dish we've ever had. It was literally a black sausage served in a black cast-iron pan with a whole roasted pepper, skin on, seeds in and stalk still attached, and with an egg cracked into the middle of it. It was roasted and then topped with a full heaped, unsifted teaspoon of pimentón. And then you mixed it all together. We've done this at Bar Lourinhã from day one. The morcilla in this recipe is like a blood cake rather than a sausage, so you don't have to mess around with sausage casings. Store-bought sausages can be used instead.

- 2 tablespoons olive oil, plus extra for drizzling
- 1 roasted Bull's Horn pepper, skin removed
- 1 slice morcilla (see below)
- 1 free-range egg
- salt, to taste
- 1 teaspoon pimentón, for dusting

MORCILLA

- 60 ml (2 fl oz/¼ cup) olive oil
- 1 onion, finely diced
- 3 garlic cloves, finely sliced
- 1 tablespoon thyme leaves
- 1 dried bay leaf
- 2 teaspoons ground cumin
- 1½ teaspoons ground allspice
- 10 g (¼ oz) salt
- 1 pinch chilli powder
- freshly ground black pepper
- 500 ml (17 fl oz/2 cups) pig's blood (see Note)
- 500 g (1 lb 2 oz) cooked short-grain rice
- 250 g (9 oz) cooked pig's head meat, finely diced (see page 60)

Preheat the oven to 160°C (320°F).

For the morcilla, heat the oil in a frying pan and gently fry the onion, garlic, thyme, bay leaf, cumin, allspice, salt, chilli powder and some pepper until very soft. Remove the bay leaf.

Add the pig's blood and cook over a very low heat until it thickens a little. Remove from the heat, then add the rice and pig's head meat. Mix well before checking the seasoning.

Line a small baking tray with baking paper and pour in the morcilla mix. Ensure the mixture spreads evenly, then place the tray in a slightly larger tray full of hot water. Transfer to the oven and bake for 30–40 minutes, or until the morcilla becomes firm. Allow to cool before cutting into 15 cm (6 in) rectangles.

Increase the oven temperature to 200°C (400°F).

Put the olive oil in the base of an ovenproof serving dish, then place the roasted pepper and morcilla next to each other, leaving a small space in between for the egg.

Place the dish on the stovetop and heat until the oil is just starting to sizzle, then crack the egg into the space between the pepper and the morcilla. Salt the egg and drizzle with a few drops of olive oil before putting in the oven. Bake for about 4–6 minutes, or until the egg is just cooked.

Dust with a teaspoon of pimentón and a drizzle of olive oil just before serving.

Note You can order pig's blood from your butcher. It normally comes in 2 litre (68 fl oz/8 cup) bottles.

Grilled Veal Tongue, Broad Beans & Yoghurt

SERVES 6

Love the tongue. We've always done it because it's Matt's favourite offal. If you can't get veal tongues, go for a baby ox tongue, but veal tongues are really beautiful with a slightly softer flavour. This whole recipe is a tribute to Samos with the yoghurt and the broad beans.

sea salt

olive oil, for drizzling

60 g (2 oz/¼ cup) yoghurt, strained for 2 hours

45 g (1½ oz/¼ cup) broad beans, blanched and podded

2 tablespoons yellow inner celery leaves

2 tablespoons flat-leaf (Italian) parsley

pinch of Aleppo pepper

TONGUE

2 veal tongues

2 carrots, roughly chopped

1 onion, roughly chopped

4 garlic cloves

3 dried bay leaves

1 tablespoon black peppercorns

250 ml (8½ fl oz/1 cup) white vinegar

3 tablespoons salt

For the tongue, rinse and wash the tongues thoroughly. Combine the tongues and all the remaining ingredients in a saucepan, then cover with cold water. Bring to the boil, then reduce the heat and simmer for about 1 hour, or until cooked. The tongue is cooked if there is little resistance when squeezed with a pair of kitchen tongs. Remove the tongues from the liquor and peel the outer layers off. Return the tongues to the liquor and transfer to the fridge to cool completely before using.

When you're ready to serve, use a long, sharp knife to slice the tongue lengthways into 5-mm (¼-in) thick slices. Season well with salt and drizzle with enough olive oil for grilling.

Heat a barbecue chargrill plate or chargrill pan to a very high heat and grill the tongue for about 4 minutes on one side before turning and grilling for another 2 minutes.

To serve, smother a serving plate with the strained yoghurt and arrange the grilled slices of tongue on top. Garnish with the broad beans, celery heart and parsley, and season generously with Aleppo pepper and a good splash of olive oil.

Veal 'Albóndigas' & Almond Sauce

SERVES 4

Albóndigas are meatballs. We serve them with a sauce that we first tasted in a place called Zapata, a tiny little corner bar in Cádiz that just served grilled meat with this almond sauce over the top. It's important to get the best-quality veal mince for the meatballs.

- 60 ml (2 fl oz/¼ cup) olive oil, plus extra for frying
- 1 onion, finely diced
- 2 garlic cloves, minced
- 2 teaspoons ground cumin
- 2 teaspoons ground fennel seeds
- 1 teaspoon ground cinnamon
- 500 g (1 lb 2 oz) minced (ground) veal
- 6 free-range eggs
- 10 g (¼ oz/⅓ cup) chopped flat-leaf (Italian) parsley
- 50 g (1¾ oz/½ cup) fine dry breadcrumbs
- 100 ml (3½ fl oz) white wine
- salt and freshly ground black pepper
- 25 g (1 oz/¼ cup) toasted flaked almonds, to garnish
- 1 teaspoon pimentón, to garnish

ALMOND SAUCE

- 500 ml (17 fl oz/2 cups) full-cream (whole) milk
- 100 g (3½ oz/1 cup) ground almonds, toasted
- 40 g (1½ oz) butter
- 30 g (1 oz) plain (all-purpose) flour
- salt and freshly ground black pepper

To make the albóndigas, heat the oil in a frying pan over a medium–low heat and gently sweat the onion for 5 minutes before adding the garlic and spices. Cook for another 4 minutes until the onion and garlic are quite soft. Remove from the heat and set aside to cool completely.

In a large mixing bowl, combine the veal mince and the cooled spiced onions. Mix well, then add the eggs, parsley, breadcrumbs and salt and pepper. Use two hands to thoroughly mix and knead the mixture – like a dough – for about 4 minutes.

Check the seasoning by cooking a small teaspoon of the mixture in a hot frying pan and tasting it. Roll the mixture into 30 g (1 oz) balls and place on a baking tray. Refrigerate for at least 30 minutes before cooking.

For the almond sauce, put the milk in a saucepan and bring to the boil. Add the ground almonds, then pour into a blender. Blend until smooth, then allow to cool.

Heat the butter in another saucepan, add the flour and cook for 4 minutes over a low heat. Add the milk mixture and season well. Cook for another 4 minutes, then remove from the heat.

Preheat the oven to 180°C (350°F).

Heat a little olive oil in a large frying pan and fry a few albóndigas at a time until evenly browned. Transfer to a small roasting tin. When all the balls have been coloured, add the wine to the frying pan and bring to the boil. Add the almond sauce, mix well, then pour over the albóndigas.

Roast in the oven, uncovered, for around 12 minutes. Remove from the tray and arrange in a serving bowl with plenty of the sauce. Garnish with a sprinkle of almonds and a light dusting of pimentón.

Grilled Lamb's Tongue, Pine Nuts & Currants

SERVES 6

This has more of a southern Italian twang to it than anything else. The sauce is fairly classic Sicilian. We love pine nuts and have burnt so many along the way trying to get the roasting just right. Make sure you spend some money on your pine nuts and check the use-by dates, because they're no good if they're rancid.

7 g (1/8 oz/1/4 cup) oregano leaves, to garnish

extra-virgin olive oil, to garnish

TONGUE

9 lamb's tongues

1 onion, roughly chopped

4 garlic cloves

3 dried bay leaves

15 g (1/2 oz/1/2 cup) oregano leaves

1 tablespoon black peppercorns

250 ml (8 1/2 fl oz/1 cup) lemon juice

3 tablespoons salt

olive oil, for chargrilling

DRESSING

1/2 red onion, finely diced

60 ml (2 fl oz/1/4 cup) merlot vinegar

35 g (1 1/4 oz/1/4 cup) currants

40 g (1 1/2 oz/1/4 cup) pine nuts, toasted

125 ml (4 fl oz/1/2 cup) blended olive oil

salt, freshly ground black pepper and caster (superfine) sugar, to taste

To prepare the tongues, rinse and wash the tongues thoroughly. Combine the tongues and all the remaining ingredients except the oil in a saucepan, then cover with cold water. Bring to the boil, then reduce the heat and simmer for about 40 minutes, or until cooked. The tongue is cooked if there is little resistance when squeezed with a pair of kitchen tongs. Remove the tongues from the liquor and peel the outer layers off. Return the tongues to the liquor and transfer to the fridge to cool completely before using.

To make the dressing, mix together the red onion and vinegar and set aside for 5 minutes to macerate. Add the currants, pine nuts and olive oil, and season well with salt, pepper and sugar to taste. Set aside.

To serve, heat a barbecue chargrill plate or a chargrill pan to a very high heat.

Slice the tongues in half lengthways, drizzle with a little olive oil and season well. Place them, sliced side down, on the grill and cook for around 3–4 minutes, or until nicely charred. Turn and do the same on the other side.

Remove the tongues from the grill and place on a serving dish. Spoon a good amount of the dressing over the top and garnish with oregano leaves and a dash of extra-virgin olive oil.

RUA
PLÍNIO
TOCA DO
RATINHO

Calves' Liver & Pimentón Sauce

SERVES 6

We were invited to a winemaker's home in Rioja. A woman lived on the estate, cooked for the family and ran the garden. She worked on this beautiful corner hearth with a big pot over the fire. Matt watched her make the sauce from go to woah. It was basically a big pot of diced-up red pepper, garlic and onion in lots of olive oil, cooked virtually at frying point. She then removed it from the heat and added vinegar and that was it. We had the sauce with fish, but it goes beautifully with meat too. Here, we have added pimentón.

- 500 g (1 lb 2 oz) calves' liver
- 3 tablespoons olive oil
- salt and freshly ground black pepper
- 125 ml (4 fl oz/½ cup) Pimentón Sauce (page 173)
- 1 tablespoon thyme leaves, to garnish

Slice the calves' liver into 1-cm (½-in) thick slices and oil and season them well. Leave to marinate for 1 hour before grilling the livers for about 3 minutes each side in a very hot chargrill pan until browned but still pink in the middle.

Arrange the livers on a plate with the pimentón sauce on top. Garnish with a loose scattering of the thyme leaves.

Portuguese Pork & Octopus Rice

SERVES 6

We ate this in a town somewhere between Lisbon and Porto on our first trip in 2005. The thing we loved about it was the baked rice – a common thread in Portuguese food, as we found out later. We've never been shy about mixing bold-flavoured seafood with big-flavoured meat, so this was our kind of dish. To get the ultimate flavour, we reserve all the cooking juices from the Twice-cooked Octopus (page 124) and use that when cooking the rice.

- 60 ml (2 fl oz/¼ cup) olive oil
- 1 onion, roughly diced
- ½ tablespoon sliced garlic
- 1 dried bay leaf
- salt and freshly ground black pepper
- 2 teaspoons pimentón
- 1 tablespoon ground cinnamon
- ½ teaspoon ground allspice
- 250 g (9 oz) pork neck, diced
- 250 g (9 oz) bomba rice
- 250 ml (8½ fl oz/1 cup) tomato juice
- 2 litres (68 fl oz/8 cups) chicken stock
- 750 g (1 lb 11 oz) Twice-cooked Octopus, chopped (page 124; see Note)
- 1 tablespoon picked lemon thyme, to garnish
- grated zest of 1 lemon, to garnish
- 12 slices finely sliced Lardo (cured pork fat) (page 54), to serve
- extra-virgin olive oil, for drizzling
- 2 teaspoons chilli flakes, to serve
- sea salt flakes

Heat the oil in a large, heavy-based saucepan and gently sweat the onion with the garlic, bay leaf and some salt and pepper.

When the onions begin to soften, add the pimentón, cinnamon, allspice and diced pork and fry for about 10 minutes over a medium heat until the pork is par-cooked.

Preheat the oven to 200°C (400°F).

Add the rice and stir well, then add the tomato juice and stock and bring to the boil. Cook until the rice just starts to soften, then remove from the heat. Add the chopped octopus and leave to cool completely to allow the rice to absorb the rest of the liquid.

Divide the rice mixture between six individual serving dishes and flatten with the back of a spoon. Bake in the oven for 12–15 minutes, or until a crust forms on top and the rice is hot.

Serve immediately, garnished with lemon thyme, lemon zest, finely sliced lardo, a drizzle of olive oil, some chilli flakes and salt.

Note Reserve the cooking juices from the Twice-cooked Octopus (page 124) for this recipe. Add the octopus cooking juices with the tomato juice and stock, and bring to the boil.

Chorizo

MAKES 2 KG (4 LB 6 OZ) SAUSAGES

We've never had bad chorizo in Spain. What you do find is varying styles and shapes. You could write a whole book on chorizo. You've got fresh, air-dried, thin ones, full links. This one is just a fresh mince sausage. Sausage-making can be tricky, but you can do it. Matt's completely self-taught – no one told him how to make a sausage, he just read books and then used his palate and trial and error. From mincing to stuffing can take about 1 hour, and it's important to cure the sausages for at least a day or two – either hang them up or lay them on a flat tray in the fridge and turn them every 12 hours.

- 25 g (1 oz) garlic
- 2 tablespoons smoked paprika
- 4 tablespoons sweet paprika
- 60 ml (2 fl oz/¼ cup) dry sherry
- ½ tablespoon freshly cracked black pepper
- 3 g (⅛ oz) salt
- 1 teaspoon caster (superfine) sugar
- 2 kg (4 lb 6 oz) free-range coarsely minced (ground) pork
- 1 length natural pork sausage casings (see Note)

Use a mortar and pestle to pound the garlic to a smooth paste. Place in a mixing bowl with the smoked paprika, sweet paprika, sherry, pepper, salt and sugar. Mix together well to form a rich red paste.

Put the pork in another largish bowl and form a well in the middle. Using gloves, add the red paste to the mince and mix together aggressively. Work the meat for 10 minutes until the paste is evenly distributed and the mince becomes tacky.

Attach the sausage casings to the nozzle on a sausage machine and gently feed the mince through, tying off the sausages at roughly 12–14 cm (4¾–5½ in) lengths by spinning the sausage in a clockwise direction.

The sausages can be cooked and eaten immediately, but, for the best results, we usually hang ours to cure and dry for around 2 days.

Note Ask your butcher for sausage casings.

Chorizo & Apple Cider

SERVES 6

We first had this in Valencia, but you will find it all over Spain. It has been on our menu from the beginning with finely sliced dried chorizo, a spritzy apple cider, fresh apple and bay leaf.

- 2 tablespoons olive oil
- 2 fresh chorizo sausages, cut into 2 cm (¾ in) slices
- 1 aged chorizo sausage, cut into ½ cm (¼ in) slices
- 1 green apple, peeled, cored and diced
- 2 garlic cloves, finely sliced
- 1 fresh bay leaf
- 150 ml (5 fl oz) dry apple cider
- salt and freshly ground black pepper
- bread, to serve

Heat the oil in a large, heavy-based saucepan and gently sear the fresh chorizo sausage on both sides until lightly golden.

Increase the heat a little and add the aged chorizo, apple, garlic and bay leaf.

Add the apple cider, season well and simmer for about 5 minutes. Serve immediately with plenty of bread.

TIP

A perfect match for this dish is a crisp, dry cider made in the Spanish style.

Twice-cooked Brisket 'Caldo Urtiga'

SERVES 6

Caldo urtiga is our rough bastardisation of a Portuguese nettle soup. We've turned it into a thick nettle sauce. It's all about a juicy piece of meat with that really punchy nettle sauce. One of the great things about Portugal is the array of greens, and we've eaten so many different varieties that we have no idea what they are called. The interesting thing here is the use of turnip as a base to thicken it up, something that they do with a lot of soups in Portugal.

125 ml (4 fl oz/½ cup) olive oil, plus extra for oiling

2 carrots, roughly diced

1 turnip, peeled and roughly diced

2 onions, roughly diced

1 teaspoon ground allspice

salt and freshly ground black pepper

500 ml (17 fl oz/2 cups) chicken stock

1 bunch nettles, hard stalks removed

ground smoked (chipotle) chilli and sea salt, to serve

fried kale leaves, to garnish

BRISKET

750 g (1 lb 11 oz) brined beef brisket

2 onions, roughly chopped

4 garlic cloves, crushed

1 star anise

1 cinnamon stick

2 bay leaves

salt and freshly ground black pepper

Preheat the oven to 170°C (340°F).

For the brisket, combine all the ingredients in a deep, ovenproof saucepan and cover with cold water. Bring to the boil, then place a piece of baking paper on the surface of the liquid and cover the pan with foil. Transfer to the oven to cook for 2 hours, or until the brisket is beginning to feel soft when squeezed with a pair of kitchen tongs. Remove from the oven and leave to cool completely in the liquor.

Heat the oil in a large frying pan and fry the carrot, turnip, onion and allspice. Season well with salt and pepper and continue cooking until the vegetables begin to soften. Add the chicken stock and bring to the boil, then reduce the heat and simmer until the vegetables begin to break down. Remove from the heat and leave to cool.

Blanch the nettles in a saucepan of boiling salted water for 2 minutes, then immediately refresh in a bowl of iced water to retain the colour. Drain and squeeze all the water from the nettles, then roughly chop.

Combine the cooked vegetables and nettles in a blender and purée until smooth. Pass through a fine-mesh sieve into a jug. The sauce should be a brilliant green colour and have a silky texture. If you have made the sauce in advance, pour into a saucepan and reheat it over a medium–low heat.

To serve, slice the brisket against the grain into large pieces and oil the meat well. Heat a barbecue chargrill plate or a chargrill pan over a very high heat and grill the brisket until dark and crispy. Season the meat with some smoked chilli and sea salt and serve over a large dollop of the caldo urtiga. Garnish with some fried kale leaves.

Pork Shoulder, Smoked Chilli & Beans

SERVES 6

Big joints of slow-cooked meat are something you'd have pretty regularly in Portugal, especially in the winter. We have used haricot beans here, but really, you can use any sort of bean that you like. The smoked chilli has come to us over time. We didn't really see it on the road but discovered it in Melbourne, from a shop called Casa Iberica. That shop has been our library of Latin flavours. A lot of our inspiration has come from walking through markets overseas, but, back home, to walk through a deli like that and see so much on every shelf, so much to learn, has been really special.

- 1 kg (2 lb 3 oz) pork shoulder, skin removed (see Note)
- 2 garlic cloves, crushed
- 2 tablespoons smoked (chipotle) chilli, ground
- 4 dried bay leaves
- 2 onions, roughly diced
- 2 Bull's Horn peppers, roughly diced
- 200 ml (7 fl oz) white wine
- 1.5 litres (51 fl oz/6 cups) chicken stock
- salt and freshly ground black pepper
- 150 g (5½ oz/¾ cup) haricot beans, soaked in cold water overnight

Preheat the oven to 180°C (350°F).

Rub the pork with the garlic and smoked chilli and combine in a deep braising tin with the bay leaves, onion, pepper, wine and chicken stock. Season well with salt and pepper. Cover with a layer of baking paper, followed by a layer of foil, then transfer to the oven. Cook for 2½ hours, or until the meat is very soft.

Remove the pork from the tray and strain the liquor into a small pot, reserving the vegetables. Add the haricot beans to the liquor and bring to the boil. Cook for about 30 minutes, until the beans are cooked through. Remove the beans using a slotted spoon and add to the vegetables.

Boil the cooking liquor to reduce it to one-third of its original volume, then add the vegetables to the pan with the beans. Roughly shred the pork and add to the pan. Stir to heat through and serve in a sharing bowl with enough liquid to make it nice and moist.

Note Ask your butcher to remove the skin from the pork shoulder for you.

Rabbit 'Migas'

SERVES 4

This is another play on another fairly traditional peasant dish in both Portugal and Spain. It's one to use up leftovers, in this case bread, to stretch out a meal. You can use any sort of meat here. We've done rabbit, pork, morcilla, chorizo and goat. It's important to layer the bread properly on the bottom of the pan so it's like a raft and ends up forming a beautiful golden crust when it's cooked that you break up and stir through just before serving.

- 60 ml (2 fl oz/¼ cup) olive oil, plus extra for greasing
- 250 g (9 oz/3 cups) torn day-old sourdough bread
- 4 braised rabbit legs, torn
- 2 garlic cloves, sliced
- 4 shallots, sliced
- 40 g (1½ oz/¼ cup) pine nuts, roasted
- 10 g (¼ oz/½ cup) flat-leaf (Italian) parsley leaves, torn
- grated zest of 1 lemon
- salt and freshly ground black pepper

Preheat the oven to 200°C (400°F).

Oil a large ovenproof frying pan and scatter the torn bread over the base followed by all the remaining ingredients except the parsley and lemon zest. Roast in the oven for 10–12 minutes, or until the bread is evenly toasted.

Add the parsley, lemon zest, some salt and pepper and enough olive oil to moisten the migas. Toss well in the pan before serving.

MOJ
VERD

Sauces & Salts

It would be fair to say that we place a strong emphasis on salt and oil. The condiments and sauces that we have developed over the years have become the lifeline of a number of dishes at the bar. These salts, sauces and oils play a big role in adding little finishing touches to a dish by tying together flavours. We are strong supporters of using local olive oil and salt.

Salsa Picante

MAKES 4 LITRES (135 FL OZ/ 16 CUPS)

This is our chilli sauce. Of course you can buy chilli sauce, but you can make your own too and it's really not that hard. Try experimenting with different types of chilli for different results. Serve it with grilled meats or fish, or use it in braises or mixed through an aioli.

250 ml (8½ fl oz/1 cup) olive oil

1 kg (2 lb 3 oz) long red chillies, tops removed (see Note)

35 g (1¼ oz/¼ cup) sea salt, plus 2 tablespoons

1 tablespoon cinnamon

6 garlic cloves, smashed

3 dried bay leaves

3 litres (101 fl oz/12 cups) white vinegar

230 g (8 oz/1 cup) caster (superfine) sugar

2 tablespoons black peppercorns

Preheat the oven to 160°C (320°F).

Combine the olive oil, chillies, 2 tablespoons sea salt, cinnamon, garlic and bay leaves in a roasting tin and roast in the oven, turning frequently, until the chillies are cooked through and very soft.

While the chillies are roasting, combine the vinegar, sugar, remaining salt and peppercorns with 500 ml (17 fl oz/2 cups) water in a saucepan and bring to a simmer over a medium heat. Simmer until the salt and sugar have dissolved.

Remove the chillies from the oven and place in a sealable bucket or large container. Pour over the vinegar mixture, place a piece of baking paper on top and press down to remove any air bubbles. Once completely cool, seal the container and leave in a cool, dark cupboard for 4 days.

Remove the chillies from the liquid and blitz to a pulp in a high-speed blender. Add small amounts of the pickling liquid to loosen the mixture. Purée to a fine, smooth paste, adding enough liquid to make a consistency that is slightly thicker than water. Divide the mixture between sterilised glass bottles or jars (see page 49) and store in the fridge for 5–6 months.

Note You can use green chillies instead, but just be aware that they can be much hotter than red chillies.

HB
HENRI
PASTIS
Suze
1889
Frangelico
LIQUEUR
Massenez
Violettes
Mendoza

Aioli

MAKES 500 G (1 LB 2 OZ)

Traditional Spanish aioli is an emulsion of garlic cloves and olive oil. For most people's palates outside of Spain, it's almost impossible to take – it burns. This is our version, derivative of French mayonnaise.

- 4 free-range egg yolks
- 1 tablespoon dijon mustard
- 4 garlic cloves, crushed
- salt and freshly ground black pepper
- 440 ml (15 fl oz) blended olive oil
- 2 tablespoons white-wine vinegar

Put the egg yolks, mustard, garlic and some salt and pepper in a food processor and blend well. Very slowly, add the olive oil, starting with just a drop at a time to allow the mixture to emulsify before adding the next drop. As the aioli thickens, you can slightly increase the rate of drips, being careful not to pour too quickly.

Once all the oil has been incorporated, the mixture should resemble a very thick mayonnaise. Add the vinegar, followed by 3 tablespoons hot water to make a shiny, smooth aioli about the consistency of cream. Check and adjust the seasoning, and store in an airtight container in the fridge for up to 2 weeks.

Note To make a thicker aioli, simply use less vinegar and water at the end.

Green Chilli Aioli

MAKES 250 G (9 OZ/1 CUP)

You can buy a green chilli sauce or make your own using the Salsa Picante recipe (page 162).

- 4 tablespoons green chilli sauce
- 1 medium green chilli, seeds removed, flesh finely chopped
- 250 g (9 oz/1 cup) Aioli, slightly thicker than normal (see opposite)

In a bowl, mix together the hot sauce, green chilli and aioli, then taste. Adjust to your preferred heat.

Smoked Chilli Aioli

MAKES 250 G (9 OZ/1 CUP)

Soak the ancho chilli in water, then blend a little bit of the water and the ancho into the aioli.

- 1 whole ancho chilli, soaked in cold water for 2 hours (see Note)
- 250 g (9 oz/1 cup) Aioli, slightly thicker than normal (see opposite)

Remove the ancho chilli from the water, reserving the liquid. Roughly remove half the seeds, then chop the flesh well.

Using a hand-held blender, blend the aioli and chilli in a bowl until smooth. Add a little of the reserved soaking water for consistency and added kick.

Note Ancho chillies are poblano chillies that have been smoked and dried.

Lemon Aioli

MAKES 600 G (1 LB 5 OZ)

Lemon aioli is a beautiful mayonnaise that cuts the garlic down with the crisp acidity from the fresh lemon. Try and use within a week or two to retain that freshness.

- 4 free-range egg yolks
- 1 tablespoon dijon mustard
- 1 garlic clove, crushed
- salt and freshly ground black pepper
- 440 ml (15 fl oz) blended olive oil
- 4 tablespoons lemon juice
- grated zest of 2 lemons

Combine the egg yolks, mustard, garlic and some salt and pepper in a food processor and blend well. Very slowly, add the olive oil, starting with just a drop at a time to allow the mixture to emulsify before adding the next drop. As the aioli thickens, you can slightly increase the rate of drips, being careful not to pour too quickly.

Once all the oil has been incorporated, the mixture should resemble a very thick mayonnaise. Add the lemon juice and zest, followed by 1 tablespoon hot water and mix well to make a shiny, smooth aioli. Check and adjust the seasoning, and store in an airtight container in the fridge for up to 10 days.

Note To make a thicker aioli, simply use less lemon juice and water at the end.

Mojo Verde

MAKES 250 ML (8½ FL OZ/ 1 CUP)

There are a lot of different green sauces in Spain. This is our version that we've used since day one. It's kind of like a chimichurri in that it uses coriander but it also has cumin, which gives it a Moorish edge. It's a vibrant sauce that goes well with meat, fish and vegetables.

60 g (2 oz/2 cups) washed coriander (cilantro) leaves and roots

50 g (1¾ oz/1 cup) English spinach

2 garlic cloves

2 teaspoons cumin seeds, crushed

50 ml (1¾ fl oz) lemon juice

50 ml (1¾ fl oz) olive oil

Combine all the ingredients in a food processor and blend until smooth. Add a little water if needed to help create a smooth paste. Store in an airtight container in the fridge for up to 1 week.

TIP

Use our Mojo Verde, or Salsa Picante (page 162), to spice up a bloody or virgin Mary.

Mojo Picon

MAKES 300 ML (10 FL OZ)

This is originally from the Canary Islands, but we first tried a version of it in Catalonia. The idea of this sauce is for it to be really, really punchy, so there's lots of garlic, cumin, chilli flakes, pimentón and vinegar. It's like you're putting all the firepower together. Use it sparingly.

50 g (1¾ oz/½ cup) stale bread, torn

1 garlic clove

2 teaspoons ground cumin

1 teaspoon chilli flakes

3 teaspoons pimentón

2 tablespoons dry-sherry vinegar

5 tablespoons blended olive oil

Soak the bread in 185 ml (6 fl oz/¾ cup) water for 15 minutes. Place all the ingredients, except the bread and water, in a blender and blitz to a smooth, runny paste.

Add the soaked bread and some of the water and blend to create a thick yet runny, brilliant red sauce.

NONINO GRAPPA
AMARO NONINO
OUZO
HENRI BARDOUIN
RITTENHOUSE RYE
JAMESON
Suze
MONTENEGRO
HAYMANS
SIPSMITH
BEEFEATER

M28·7
STORAGE BARREL

Salts

Salt is an important element of a number of our dishes. Adding flavoured salts is something we have always done and injects a final punch to a dish. We like to make these in small quantities to retain freshness and store them in sealed containers.

PIMENTÓN SALT

In a clean, dry bowl, mix together 35 g (1¼ oz/ ¼ cup) sea salt flakes with 2 tablespoons pimentón. Mix well, being careful not to damage the salt flakes.

CHILLI SALT

Mix together 35 g (1¼ oz/ ¼ cup sea salt flakes with 2 teaspoons chilli flakes and 1 teaspoon dried thyme leaves and mix well.

CHIPOTLE SALT

Roast and grind 3 smoked (chipotle) chillies to make a fine powder. Mix this with 35 g (1¼ oz/¼ cup) sea salt flakes.

Store your salts in airtight containers and use within 1 month.

Pimentón Sauce

MAKES APPROX. 1 LITRE (34 FL OZ/ 4 CUPS)

This is the sauce that we use with the grilled calves' liver recipe, but it goes well with fish and vegetables too.

- 2 Bull's Horn peppers
- 250 ml (8½ fl oz/1 cup) olive oil
- 2 teaspoons salt
- 2 garlic cloves, finely sliced
- 2 shallots, finely sliced
- 4 tablespoons red-wine vinegar
- 1 tablespoon pimentón
- 2 tablespoons thyme leaves

Remove the tops and seeds from the peppers and dice the flesh into 1 cm (½ in) squares.

Combine the peppers with the olive oil and salt in a saucepan and slowly bring to the boil. Simmer, stirring continuously, so the peppers do not catch and burn on the bottom. When the peppers have softened and shrunk, remove the pan from the heat. Add the garlic and shallot and mix well. Allow to cool completely before adding the vinegar, pimentón and thyme. Stir well and store in a sterilised glass jar (see page 49) in the fridge for up to 2 weeks.

Chilli Oil

MAKES 100 ML (3½ FL OZ)

This is a great way to spice up a dish, but it also adds a smoky paprika edge. Perfect for the King Prawn & Pork Pincho (page 28).

- 1 tablespoon spicy pimentón
- 100 ml (3½ fl oz) olive oil

Mix the pimentón and olive oil in a bowl until smooth, then store in a sterilised glass jar or bottle (see page 49) for up to 2 months.

Dulces

The sweet finishers at Bar Lourinhã have always been about speed of service and few ingredients with a heavy emphasis on sugar. Nuts, citrus, vanilla and seasonal fruit always play a major role in our dessert selection. We like to keep things simple at this end of the meal; there is no reason why the combination of a few sweet ingredients can't be as good, if not better, than a complicated dessert. It's a time to wind down, refresh and indulge without bombarding the palate with too many flavours.

Pomegranate Crema, Pistachio Praline

SERVES 8

We ate heaps of pomegranates in Samos and saw them all over the place in Spain and Portugal. We love the combination of pomegranate and pistachio – they're pretty much best buddies. We did a lot of different desserts in Samos playing around with these two ingredients. When pomegranates are in season, you'll always see them on our menu.

pomegranate seeds, to serve

PISTACHIO PRALINE

75 g (2¾ oz/½ cup) pistachio nuts, roasted

345 g (12 oz/1½ cups) caster (superfine) sugar

CREMA

1 litre (34 fl oz/4 cups) thickened cream

115 g (4 oz/½ cup) caster (superfine) sugar

¼ vanilla pod, split and scraped

3 gelatine leaves, soaked

2 tablespoons pomegranate molasses

LEMON SYRUP

6 tablespoons Sugar Syrup (see right)

2 tablespoons lemon juice

To make the pistachio praline, place the pistachios on a baking tray lined with baking paper and set aside.

Put the sugar in a small, heavy-based saucepan and add enough water to cover the sugar. Stir gently, then place over a high heat. Cook until the sugar begins to change colour, trying not to stir or allow the sugar to crystallise. Once you have an even, dark caramel, carefully pour the mixture over the pistachios. Leave to cool completely before roughly chopping with a knife.

For the crema, combine the cream, sugar and vanilla in a heavy-based saucepan set over a low heat. Heat gently, to no more than 50°C (122°F), and stir occasionally to help the sugar dissolve. Remove from the heat and allow to steep for 5 minutes, then squeeze any excess water from the gelatine leaves and stir them into the mixture with the pomegranate molasses. Stir well, then pass the crema through a fine-mesh sieve and pour into serving bowls. Allow to cool and set in the fridge before serving.

While the crema sets, make the lemon syrup. Combine the sugar syrup and lemon juice in a bowl and refrigerate until ready to serve.

To serve, sprinkle a generous amount of the chopped praline, lemon syrup and pomegranate seeds on top of the crema.

SUGAR SYRUP

Prepare a sugar syrup by combing equal parts caster (superfine) sugar and boiling water. Stir until the sugar has dissolved.

Leche Frita

SERVES 8

Who doesn't like fried custard? It's just the best. We had this for the first time in Barcelona and we really loved it because it kind of reminded us of the Greek dessert galaktoboureko, the custard wrapped in filo and then baked.

1 litre (34 fl oz/4 cups) blended olive oil, for deep-frying and greasing

250 ml (8½ fl oz/1 cup) thickened cream, to serve

icing (confectioners') sugar, for dusting

CUSTARD

750 ml (25½ fl oz/3 cups) full-cream (whole) milk

grated zest of 2 lemons

1 cinnamon stick, broken in half

5 free-range egg yolks

50 g (1¾ oz) caster (superfine) sugar

90 g (3 oz/¾ cup) cornflour (cornstarch)

CRUMB

150 g (5½ oz/1 cup) plain (all-purpose) flour

2 free-range eggs, beaten

250 g (9 oz/2½ cups) fine dry breadcrumbs

To make the custard, put the milk in a saucepan and bring to the boil, then remove from the heat and add the lemon zest and cinnamon. Leave to steep for 15 minutes, then strain, discarding the solids, and set aside.

Beat the egg yolks in a mixing bowl until pale, then add the sugar and the cornflour and whisk to a smooth paste. Gradually add the milk in a steady stream, whisking constantly. Return the mixture to the saucepan and place it back over a medium heat. Cook for about 7–9 minutes until thick, stirring constantly. Pour into a well-oiled tray to cool. Once cool, cut, roll and weigh the custard into 50 g (1¾ oz) balls.

To crumb the custard balls, dredge them well in the flour, then drop them into the beaten egg and roll them in the crumbs. Transfer to a plate and chill in the fridge until ready to serve.

When you're ready to serve, heat the olive oil in a large, heavy-based saucepan or deep-fryer until it reaches 160°C (320°F) on a cooking thermometer. Once hot, fry about six balls of custard at a time until golden. Transfer to paper towels to drain.

Pour the thickened cream on a serving plate and arrange the leche frita on top. Dust with icing sugar to serve.

Sweet Fried Queso Fresco & Chocolate

SERVES 8

This is loosely based on a southern Italian dessert. We make this with chocolate because it tastes really beautiful when you put it in the deep-fryer, especially with the cheese. It oozes little pockets of chocolate through the cheese.

250 g (9 oz/1 cup) ricotta

75 g (2¾ oz) caster (superfine) sugar

1 free-range egg

75 g (2¾ oz/½ cup) dark chocolate (70 per cent), chopped

100 g (3½ oz/⅔ cup) self-raising flour

blended olive oil, for deep-frying

100 ml (3½ fl oz) thickened cream

icing (confectioners') sugar, for dusting

Mix together the ricotta, sugar, egg and chocolate in a bowl, thenadd the flour. Gently mix until just combined.

Roll the mixture into 35 g (1¼ oz) balls. Add enough oil for deep-frying to a large, heavy-based saucepan or deep-fryer and heat the oil until it reaches 170°C (340°F) on a cooking thermometer. Working in batches, fry the balls until golden, then remove and drain on paper towels.

Smear the cream on a serving plate and arrange the balls on top. Dust with icing sugar to serve.

CARDINAL MENDOSA

Originated in 1887 by Sanchez Romate Hermanos in Jerez, this luscious brandy is matured in Olorosso and Pedro Ximénez sherry casks and is our go-to drink at the end of a meal.

Olive Oil Cake, Yoghurt Sorbet

MAKES 1 LARGE OR 10 SMALL CAKES

This recipe is based on a cake we had in Naples with the family. We love the mix of olive oil and lemon to create this very simple torte.

- cooking spray, for greasing
- 10 free-range eggs, separated
- grated zest and juice of 2 lemons
- 345 g (12 oz/1½ cups) caster (superfine) sugar
- 375 ml (12½ fl oz/1½ cups) olive oil
- 300 g (10½ oz/2 cups) plain (all-purpose) flour, sifted
- pinch of salt
- 250 g (9 oz/1⅔ cups) strawberries, finely sliced, to serve
- 60 ml (2 fl oz/¼ cup) Sugar Syrup, to serve (page 176)

YOGHURT SORBET

- 250 g (9 oz/1 cup) natural-set yoghurt
- 250 ml (8½ fl oz/1 cup) thickened cream
- 150 g (5½ oz) caster (superfine) sugar

Preheat the oven to 180°C (350°F). Spray a 25 cm (10 in) springform cake tin with cooking spray. Or, if you're making 10 small cakes, use a muffin tin with 7-cm (2¾-in) diameter holes.

Beat the egg yolks, zest and sugar in a large bowl until thick and pale. Add the lemon juice and continue beating. Slowly add the olive oil and beat until combined (the mixture may appear separated). Using a wooden spoon, gently stir in the flour (do not beat) until just combined.

In another large bowl, whisk the egg whites with the salt until soft peaks form. Gently fold one-third of the whites into the yolk mixture to lighten, then fold in the remaining whites gently but thoroughly.

Pour the cake mixture into the tin and bake for 30 minutes for a large cake and 20 minutes for smaller cakes, until puffed and golden. The cake is ready when a skewer inserted in the middle comes out clean.

While the cake is baking, prepare the yoghurt sorbet. Whisk together the yoghurt, cream and sugar until combined. Place in an ice-cream maker and churn according to the manufacturer's instructions. Freeze the sorbet for up to 1 week, but no longer, otherwise it will become too hard.

To serve, mix the strawberries and sugar syrup in a bowl, then arrange on top of the cake. Drizzle with a little extra syrup and serve with a dollop of yoghurt sorbet.

La MALDICION

Arroz Doce, Rhubarb & Roasted Walnuts

SERVES 8

Matt grew up with really, really bad rice pudding as a kid and absolutely hated it. And then, much later, we ate it in Portugal and he said: Why is it so much better? Then we realised it was because they put so much sugar in it. This recipe comes from a traditional Portuguese version, minus about two-thirds of the sugar.

200 g (7 oz) medium-grain rice

500 ml (17 fl oz/2 cups) full-cream (whole) milk

150 ml (5 fl oz) thickened cream

1 cinnamon stick

grated zest of 1 lemon

½ vanilla bean, seeds scraped

75 g (2¾ oz) caster (superfine) sugar

3 free-range egg yolks

30 g (1 oz/¼ cup) chopped roasted walnuts, to serve

POACHED RHUBARB

500 g (1 lb 2 oz) caster (superfine) sugar

2 star anise

1 bunch rhubarb

Boil the rice in a generous amount of salted water until just cooked. Drain, return to the saucepan and set aside.

Combine the milk, cream, cinnamon, lemon zest and vanilla seeds and pod in a large saucepan and bring to the boil, then remove from the heat and leave to steep for 15 minutes. Strain the milk into the rice, discarding the solids, then stir in the sugar and egg yolks. Serve warm, or refrigerate and gently reheat when needed.

For the rhubarb, combine the sugar and star anise with 750 ml (25½ fl oz/3 cups) water in a large saucepan and bring to the boil.

Trim the rhubarb and wash well. Cut the stalks into 10 cm (4 in) lengths and place in the hot sugar syrup. Simmer for 3–4 minutes, then remove from the heat and leave to cool in the syrup. Once cool, refrigerate until ready to serve.

To serve, divide the warm rice pudding between serving bowls, top with the rhubarb and a little syrup, and the roasted walnuts.

Blanca's Alfajores

MAKES 15–20 BISCUITS

Blanca is the mother of a friend of ours from South America. Before we first opened we spent a bit of time with him and his family and Blanca would make these beautiful biscuits called alfajores. Traditionally, they're from Argentina. Blanca was from Paraguay and her husband was from Argentina. Before they came to Australia, her mother-in-law pulled her aside and gave her a book on Argentinian cooking. She said to Blanca: 'If you don't know these recipes, my son will either die or leave you.' Blanca cooked them, but she cooked them her way and the lightness of her biscuit was really beautiful. You use these to sandwich a blob of dulce de leche, which is Blanca's recipe as well.

- 200 g (7 oz) butter
- 300 g (10½ oz) caster (superfine) sugar
- 2 free-range egg yolks
- 2 free-range eggs
- grated zest of 1 lemon
- 225 g (8 oz/1½ cups) plain (all-purpose) flour, sifted, plus extra for dusting
- 310 g (11 oz/2½ cups) cornflour (cornstarch), sifted
- 2 teaspoons baking powder, sifted
- 1 × 400 g (14 oz) tin sweetened condensed milk
- 90 g (3 oz/1 cup) dessicated coconut, for rolling

Beat the butter and sugar in a food processor until light and creamy. Add the egg yolks and whole eggs followed by the lemon zest. Quickly add the dry ingredients, being careful not to overwork the mixture. Wrap the dough in plastic wrap and allow to rest in the fridge for about 1 hour before rolling.

Preheat a fan-forced oven to 150°C (300°F) or heat a conventional oven to 170°C (340°F).

Roll out the dough on a lightly floured surface to ½ cm (¼ in) thick. Using a 3 cm (1¼ in) round cutter, cut out the alfajores. Place the biscuits on a baking tray lined with baking paper and bake for 10–15 minutes, or until cooked but not coloured. Transfer to a wire rack to cool completely.

To make the dulce de leche (see Note), open the tin of sweetened condensed milk and place the tin in a saucepan. Pour in enough cold water to come three-quarters of the way up the side of the tin. Bring to the boil, then reduce the heat and allow to simmer for 4 hours, replacing any water that evaporates. Turn off the heat and leave to cool completely before removing from the saucepan. The dulce de leche should be dark-brown in colour and thick, like a paste.

Spread the base of one biscuit with dulce de leche and press another biscuit against it. Spread the dulce de leche around the rim of the biscuit, then roll in coconut.

Note Dulce de leche is an Argentinean caramel sauce. This recipe calls for a very thick dulce de leche firm enough to be sandwiched between two biscuits.

Churros & Dulce de Leche

SERVES 6

When we first arrived in Valencia, we ordered churros and they arrived plain with nothing on them. This was how we discovered that churros could be sweet or savoury and you have to let them know which one you want. Now, churros have taken over the world and can be a bit of a dirty word since they've been franchised and commercialised, but they're so great (and impressive) to make at home. Normally they're served with chocolate on the side, but dulce de leche has always been our thing.

DULCE DE LECHE

400 g (14 oz/1¾ cups) caster (superfine) sugar

1 vanilla bean, split

3 litres (101 fl oz/12 cups) full-cream (whole) milk

CHURROS

300 g (10½ oz/2 cups) cake flour

pinch of salt

¼ teaspoon baking powder

115 g (4 oz/½ cup) caster (superfine) sugar

1 tablespoon ground cinnamon, preferably freshly ground

blended olive oil, for deep-frying

For the dulce de leche, put the sugar in a heavy, wide-based saucepan and lie the vanilla bean flat in the bottom.

Set the pan over a high heat and cook until the sugar starts to melt. Continue cooking, trying not to stir or move the mixture, until the sugar turns an even, dark caramel colour.

Carefully pour in the milk and stir to break up the toffee as much as possible. Bring the mixture back to the boil, then reduce the heat to a steady simmer and cook the mixture until it has the consistency of a sauce. Strain and immediately transfer it to the fridge to cool quickly.

To make the churros, sift the flour, salt and baking powder together, then set aside.

Bring 625 ml (21 fl oz/2½ cups) water to the boil, then turn off the heat and add the flour mixture. Mix continuously until combined, being careful not to overwork the batter. Remove from the heat and rest for a few minutes, then place in a churros maker (see Note) and pipe into lengths onto a baking tray lined with baking paper. Allow to cool completely before cutting into 15 cm (6 in) pieces.

Combine the sugar and cinnamon in a bowl.

Add enough oil for deep-frying to a large, heavy-based saucepan or deep-fryer and heat the oil until it reaches 165°C (330°F) on a cooking thermometer. Fry the churros until crisp and golden, then remove and toss in the sugar and cinnamon mixture to coat. Serve with the dulce de leche.

Note A churros maker, or churrería, is a plastic or metal pipe with a fitted nozzle at one end and a turning handle at the other that forces the churros through the nozzle into lengths. You can purchase churros makers from good Latin food stores or cookware shops. Alternatively, you can use a piping (icing) bag and your choice of nozzle to pipe the churros, but it's a difficult process.

Harlem End

30 ml (1 fl oz) dark rum

30 ml (1 fl oz) freshly brewed espresso

15 ml (½ fl oz) Caffè Moka Liqueur (see Note)

15 ml (½ fl oz) Pedro Ximénez

ice cubes, for shaking

3 coffee beans, to garnish

Combine all the ingredients in a cocktail shaker and top with ice. Shake vigorously for 10 seconds, then strain into a Coupe glass and garnish with the coffee beans.

Note Caffè Moka is fine liqueur distilled from espresso by the famous Italian distiller, Varnelli.

AMARO

Amaro Nonnino is a perfectly balanced mix of herbs and grappa from the Friuli region of Italy. It is perfect neat, over ice or with a slice of orange, and has a wonderfully sweet and bitter flavour.

Torta Naranja

MAKES 8

Orange cake is a classic dish of the south of Spain. Oranges and almonds go brilliantly together. We serve this cake with an orange syrup over the top alongside thick cream and candied clementines. If you can't find clementines, any form of candied citrus will be perfect.

4 free-range eggs, separated

160 g (5½ oz) caster (superfine) sugar

grated zest of 2 oranges

pinch of salt

160 g (5½ oz) ground almonds

50 g (1¾ oz/⅓ cup) plain (all-purpose) flour

3 candied clementines, sliced, to serve

250 ml (8½ fl oz/1 cup) thick cream, to serve

ORANGE SYRUP

1 cinnamon stick

juice of 4 oranges

juice of 1 lemon

115 g (4 oz/½ cup) caster (superfine) sugar

Preheat the oven to 170°C (340°F).

Whisk the egg yolks, sugar and orange zest in a bowl until the mixture is pale and the sugar has dissolved. In another bowl, beat the egg whites with the salt until soft peaks form.

Gently fold the ground almonds and flour into the egg yolk mixture, followed by the egg whites. Pour into eight 6 × 9 cm (2½ × 3½ in) rectangular cake tins. Bake for 25 minutes, or until slightly firm and a skewer inserted in the middle of a cake comes out clean.

Remove from the oven and leave the cakes to cool in their tins on a wire rack for 10 minutes before removing.

In the meantime, prepare the syrup. Combine all the ingredients in a saucepan and bring to the boil. Remove from the heat and leave to cool completely, then strain the syrup through a fine-mesh sieve, discarding the solids, and set aside until ready to serve. Once the cakes are cool, remove them from the tins and place in a deep tray. Pour a generous amount of the syrup over the top, allowing the cakes to soak in the syrup.

Arrange the cakes on individual serving plates and spoon another tablespoon of syrup over the top. Decorate with slices of candied clementine and serve with a dollop of thick cream.

'Torta de Queso', Figs & Almonds

SERVES 8

Cheesecake. It's been a bit of a fad in Spain for a while. There is cream cheese involved and this is the only time Matt's used cream cheese in his life. We also add lemon zest, mascarpone and Liquor 43, the Spanish vanilla liqueur. We only make it when figs are in season because they go so well with this combo.

- cooking spray, for greasing
- 250 g (9 oz) cream cheese
- 115 g (4 oz/½ cup) caster (superfine) sugar
- 2 free-range eggs
- 1 free-range egg yolk
- grated zest and juice of 1 lemon (about 50 ml/1¾ fl oz juice)
- 200 g (7 oz) mascarpone
- 2 tablespoons Liquor 43
- 3 figs, roughly torn
- 60 ml (2 fl oz/¼ cup) Sugar Syrup (page 176)
- 25 g (1 oz/¼ cup) flaked almonds, toasted

Preheat the oven to 160°C (320°F). Grease eight 2 × 2 × 9 cm (¾ × ¾ × 3½ in) rectangular rubber moulds with cooking spray.

Combine the cream cheese and sugar in a food processor and pulse until combined. Add the eggs and the lemon zest and juice, and pulse until incorporated. Finally, add the mascarpone and Liquor 43 and pulse again. Spoon the mixture into the moulds until they are completely full.

Transfer the moulds to a deep baking tray and fill the tray with boiling water to just below the top of the moulds. Bake for 25–30 minutes, or until the cheesecake feels firm.

To serve, combine the figs and sugar syrup in a bowl and leave to macerate for 5 minutes. Arrange each torta on a plate with the figs and sprinkle with the toasted almonds.

Molotov & Blood-orange Caramel

MAKES 8

Molotov is a traditional Portuguese dessert. Think of an Eton Mess, but with a soft rather than a hard meringue. Make sure to pour over plenty of caramel so there's a pool of sauce for the meringue to swim in.

180 g (6½ oz) free-range egg whites, at room temperature

pinch of fine salt

145 g (5 oz/⅔ cup) caster (superfine) sugar

cooking spray, for greasing

grated zest of 1 orange, to garnish

BLOOD-ORANGE CARAMEL

345 g (12 oz/1½ cups) caster (superfine) sugar

500 ml (17 fl oz/2 cups) blood-orange juice

ORANGE CHANTILLY

150 ml (5 fl oz) thickened cream

¼ teaspoon vanilla extract

grated zest of 1 orange

50 g (1¾ oz) caster (superfine) sugar

Preheat a fan-forced oven to 160°C (320°F) or heat a conventional oven to 180°C (350°F).

To make the molotov, whip the egg whites in the bowl of a stand mixer fitted with the whisk attachment (see Note). Once they become a little bit fluffy, add the salt and continue mixing. Gradually add the sugar (1 teaspoon at a time), whisking constantly, until all the sugar has been incorporated. The mixture should resemble a very white and stiff meringue.

Grease six 6 × 9 cm (2½ × 3½ in) baking moulds with cooking spray, then fill the moulds to the top with the meringue. Flatten the tops with the back of a wet spoon. Transfer the moulds to a deep baking tray and fill the tray with boiling water to just below the top of the moulds. Carefully place in the oven and bake for 30–40 minutes until the meringue is cooked and lightly browned on top.

While the meringues are cooking, make the caramel. Put the sugar in a clean, wide-based saucepan, making sure the sugar is evenly spread over the base of the pan. Place over a medium–high heat. Do not move or stir the sugar, but pay close attention to it melting and changing colour. When it becomes more liquidy, gently agitate the pan to ensure an even colour on the caramel. Once it turns a dark golden colour, pour in the orange juice and bring back to the boil, then reduce the heat to low and simmer for 10 minutes. Strain and set aside to cool.

To make the orange Chantilly, combine all the ingredients in a bowl and whisk until stiff. Fit a piping (icing) bag with a fine star nozzle and fill the bag with the cream. Refrigerate until ready to serve.

To serve, place the molotovs on a plate and pour a very generous amount of the caramel over the top. Pipe the cream in very small rosettes to completely cover the molotov. Finish with a light dusting of orange zest.

Note It is very important that the mixing bowl and whisk attachment for the meringue are spotlessly clean and completely dry before you start.

UINTA
VALE
MARIA

BAR
Lourinhã

About the authors

Matt McConnell

Matt is the executive chef and co-owner of the popular Bar Lourinhã. He has been at the centre of Melbourne's thriving bar and dining culture for the past two decades, and is one of the city's most loved and respected chefs. After an extended journey through Europe, where he spent time with family exploring the simple beauty found in shared farm feasts and country cooking, Matt returned home to Melbourne in 2006 to open Bar Lourinhã with his business partner and wife, Jo Gamvros. Matt's energy and inspiration is centred around enjoying flavours in a fun and casual setting that reflects the Iberian and Mediterranean passion and spirit for eating and drinking. In 2017, Bar Lourinhã was awarded one chef's hat in the *Good Food Guide's* first national edition.

Jo Gamvros

Jo is co-owner of Bar Lourinhã, where she runs the front-of-house team. She has worked in Melbourne as a hospitality professional for more than 30 years. Jo studied a Bachelor of Photography with Honours at RMIT and has exhibited solo and joint shows throughout her career. She has worked as a freelance photographer for Fairfax Media and other national publications. Jo's passion for shooting markets and food cultures around the world is reflected in the dining ethos at Bar Lourinhã, where every detail – from the menu to the atmosphere – tells a story. As a passionate antique collector, Jo also curates the bar's 'walls of madness' to create a space that is as visually rich as it is welcoming.

RINCÓN Del 2
白州

Acknowledgements

To our parents, Maria, Peter and Margaret, for their continued support and encouragement to follow our dreams.

Thank you to our little squids, Remi and Dion, who are the best travel partners.

Many thanks to the extended family throughout Greece and Italy who have shared their homes, kitchens and stories with us.

Thank you to the entire Bar Lourinhã team over the years, especially our restaurant manager, Rui Lourenço.

To our valued supply chain of farmers, fishermen, butchers, providores and all who work so hard to keep the good stuff coming.

And also to Michael Harden, Trisha Garner, Mark Roper and the Hardie Grant team.

Index

a

B

C

N

O

P

R

S

GOOD
TIMES

This edition published in 2026 by Hardie Grant Books, an imprint of Hardie Grant Publishing

First published in 2018

Hardie Grant Books (Melbourne)
Wurundjeri Country
Level 11, 36 Wellington Street
Collingwood, Victoria 3066

Hardie Grant North America
2912 Telegraph Ave
Berkeley, California 94705

hardiegrant.com/books

Hardie Grant acknowledges the Traditional Owners of the Country on which we work, the Wurundjeri People of the Kulin Nation and the Gadigal People of the Eora Nation, and recognises their continuing connection to the land, waters and culture. We pay our respects to their Elders past and present.

A catalogue record for this book is available from the National Library of Australia

Lourinhã
ISBN 978 1 76145 120 1

10 9 8 7 6 5 4 3 2 1

Head of Editorial: Jasmin Chua
Project Editor & Editor: Andrea O'Connor
Creative Director: Kristin Thomas
Designer: Trisha Garner, Celia Mance
Illustrator: Emily O'Neill
Photographer: Mark Roper
Location Photography: Jojogamvros
Stylist: Stephanie Stamatis
Head of Production: Todd Rechner

Colour reproduction by Splitting Image Colour Studio
Printed in China by Leo Paper Products Ltd.

The paper this book is printed on is from FSC®-certified forests and other sources. FSC® promotes environmentally responsible, socially beneficial and economically viable management of the world's forests.

This book uses 15 ml (1/2 fl oz) tablespoons; cooks with 20 ml (3/4 fl oz) tablespoons should be scant with their tablespoon measurements.

RINCÓN Del 2x4
ARGENTINA
TANGO
AMARO NONINO
Frangelico
43
Havana Club
Sagatiba
CHARTREUSE
SAMOS
OUZO
PASTIS
SUZE
CAMPARI
APEROL
HAYMANS
BEEFEATER